In Wisdom and Grace

Raymond J. Stovich, Ph.D.

Sheed & Ward

Copyright© 1988
Raymond J. Stovich

Sheed & Ward™ is a service of National Catholic Reporter Publishing
Company, Inc.

Library of Congress Catalog Card Number: 88-61711

ISBN: 1-55612-115-6

Published by: Sheed & Ward
               115 E. Armour Blvd. P.O. Box 419492
               Kansas City, MO 64141-4292

To order, call: (800) 333-7373

Contents

I dedicate this book to my
grandparents, Stanley & Wiktoria
Kurcz and John & Teofila Stovich,
who first taught me the Wisdom and
Grace of life's latter years...
and to those people, my clients,
who continued that lesson...may
this work benefit them and all
sentient beings.

Acknowledgements

Imagine, if you will, trying to write this book, or any book, on your own. Indeed, how absolutely ridiculous! So, at the risk of offending many people who have helped bring this book to life, I wish to offer special mention to a few key persons.

First and foremost, my profound thanks go to the hundreds of people who have let me enter into their lives. Each day people have shared memories, dreams, fears, hopes, joys and regrets with me, frequently opening areas of their lives never before (or again) shared with another. I have tried my best to hear them and to help them realize their own human beauty, power and dignity. This book is truly a book of their stories. (I have changed details, combined stories or shifted them around a bit in order to protect the identity of each individual.)

The original form of this book was my Doctoral Dissertation for the California Institute of Transpersonal Psychology. Invaluable assistance in clarifying my thinking was offered me by my committee, Drs. Robert Frager, Megan Nolan and Thomas Moore. I expecially thank Tom Moore for help above and beyond the call of duty, including support when I was near despair, a push when things were going too smoothly and words and phrases—lots of words and phrases. Tom was indeed a midwife to my Dissertation. I also wish to thank the Polish Union of America and the Kosciuszko Foundation for grants which came at critical times, enabling me to continue my own work.

And then came the rewrites. And Diane Russell's typing and Robert Clark's encouragement and critiques. This book couldn't have happened without them. Thanks to both. Thanks to audiences at lectures and conferences, people who listened to my ideas, pointed out their strengths and challenged them when sloppy or ill-formed.

And to Bob Heyer of Sheed & Ward who not only believed in this book enough to risk printing it, but also helped guide it along every step of the way. Authors write books, editors make them happen! And to June Williams, also of Sheed & Ward, whose courtesy and kindness removed obstacles along the way.

And to Barbara Fink and Heide Didwiszu who selflessly toiled on that most thankless of jobs, proofreading.

Finally, I wish to thank Linda C. Subia, a good friend, who helped in every phase of this work. Without her support and encouragement, her critiques and suggestions, and her belief that I have something worthwhile to say, this book would be only halfway through its first draft stage.

I am sure that if I incorporated more suggestions from these fine people this book would be more accurate and better written, but I didn't and only I can shoulder blame for that, as well as for any other errors found in this book.

Introduction

Many older people find themselves in dead-end streets. In searching for ways to help people out of this stagnation, the author found that the use of creative and transforming images could open the doors to satisfactory living. He then realized that these methods could help any of us come to wholeness and fulfillment. He shares his findings in a clear and practical way in the pages that follow.

In Wisdom and Grace is a book about growth, healing, and fulfillment. The reader is, first of all, introduced to the idea of the wounded healer, the only healer whom we can trust. We are then led to consider the place of reflection over memories if we are to change our course forward. We can only do this as we take time and enter the silence in which our lives lie before us, crying for redirection. So few of us know the healing power of silence.

As we enter the inner world of silence we need the direction of religion and of love. Religion is the accumulated wisdom of humankind about how we can relate to The Other safely. We can find destructive elements within the silence as well as the Divine Lover who seeks to love us and bring us to our fulfillment in a land more kind than home, more large than earth.

The great religions of humankind, and Christianity in particular, give us directions on this journey.

As we come to know The Other we find that the center and source of our being and reality is love, self-giving caring. This love is nowhere better portrayed than in the teachings, stories and life of Jesus of Nazareth. Unless our lives are seeking to express this kind of love, we don't move toward creativity and wholeness. The author points out that this movement toward wisdom and grace is as much a dance, divine play, as it is a serious undertaking.

We are reminded again and again how much we can learn from the aged as we seriously, playfully take up the journey toward wisdom and grace. The author calls us to understand, to listen to stories, and join in the fascinating calling of coming to greater joys than we had dreamed existed. Not only are we called by these pages, we are given examples and concrete directions on how we can make our way toward that goal.

Morton Kelsey

Instructions for the Exercises Found in This Book

Most of the chapters of this book contain an "exercise" which has been designed to enable you to relate the material found in this book to your own personal life experiences. These exercises are primarily a visualization style of meditation. It is best to do each exercise in a quiet place free of all distractions. It is also best to be in a relaxed state when you try each exercise.

The easiest way to do each exercise is by using a prerecorded tape. For instructions on purchasing a professionally recorded tape of these exercises, please turn to the last page of this book. Without a tape, you may want to read each exercise a few times before you try it. Then get relaxed and read the exercise to yourself very slowly, stopping frequently to perform the visualization as directed. You may also try working with a friend ' or a small group, taking turns as reader and meditator. This approach offers the benefits of mutual sharing. Many find that repeating the meditation after sharing the results of a previous attempt deepens the experience.

Although these visualizations are quite easy to perform, if you are not familiar with this kind of work you may need a few practice sessions with each visualization before you begin to experience its full value. Be gentle with yourself. Treat each exercise as an experiment which has no predetermined outcome. Do each experiment to discover its results for that specific time. Don't be surprised if you get different results each time you try an experiment, or if the results are always the same. If nothing "happens" after a few tries, don't be discouraged—move on and return to that exercise at some later date. With some practice and a little patience you will discover that these visualizations will lead you to a greater familiarity with your inner life and help you to develop a perspective which will open you to the depth dimensions of your daily life.

1

In Wisdom and Grace

1.

It was not that he wanted to lie.

He told me about that boy, Robert, a very strong willed young buck. He told me about his fights with his parents, fights the whole village knew about. All of the villagers spoke about Robert, and most tried their best to avoid him. Those of a more philosophical nature wondered how this childhood waywardness would influence his adult life. As if trying to convince themselves, they kept repeating that he was just burning it out of his system.

One day Robert's parents asked him to weed the garden, a task Robert despised. He refused. This was the last straw. His father became so enraged that he lifted his hand to hit the boy, but Robert beat him to it. Smack! His father had a handprint across the face and Robert lay on the floor, dead. God had struck him down.

A few days after the burial the village grave digger noticed something unusual in the graveyard. It was a hand, a young boy's hand, sticking out of a new grave. Indeed it was Robert's. The village was in an uproar. Finally the Mayor, the Priest and a few elders gathered in conference and issued their commands. Robert's father was called upon to act, and this time he could not refuse. With the entire village present, this man, whose hair had turned almost completely white in the past few days, walked up to the grave, raised his own hand and struck the cold hand of his son as it protruded from beyond life, saying, "I am your father and you will obey me." Immediately the ground shook, opened and accepted the hand of this youth to its final resting place.

When he told me this story my grandfather had no intention of lying to me. He believed it had actually taken place in his village, just as his grandfather had told him it did. It was only years later when I was in graduate school that I discovered the truth. I read this story, and many others of the stories told to me by my grandfather, in a book—a book written by the brothers Grimm.

My grandfather had given me many precious gifts, not all of material value, and had passed on much wisdom, but nothing was as important as that story. For untold time this story, and others, were passed from generation to generation by word of mouth. In this living tradition of oral storytelling the values, beliefs and self-identities of our people were handed down. My grandfather placed me into that tradition. He gave me my psychic roots.

2.

The Wise Old Man is a figure that still haunts us, although perhaps more in imagination than in daily life. But at one time it was different. In traditional societies the elders held a special position. They were the wise ones, holders of the Wisdom of the tribe. They settled disputes, divided land and property, approved or disapproved marriages, and interpreted dreams. Frequently they were the intermediaries between the people and their gods. Frequently they were healers. Men and women of power. They kept the myths, those stories which contained the deepest understandings and identities of a people, and passed them on.

People were respected for their age. Not simply because they lasted as many days, years and months as they did, but because age stood for something. Age stood for Wisdom, Wisdom gained from Experience. Life is filled with experiences. Every moment of every day is an experience, but that does not account for Wisdom. More was needed. Life had to be lived fully, consciously. It wasn't enough just to walk through the woods. One had to keep awake, watch for the signs of the changing patterns of animal migration, watch for new locations of roots and herbs, and remember them. And yet even more was needed.

Rainer Maria Rilke, a German poet who had a tremendous influence on modern poetry, in describing the process of creating verse inadvertently gave a description of the transformation of experiences and memories into Wisdom. Rilke wrote that we must experience a full life—not as passive witnesses to things and events, but as active participants. We must live each moment as fully as we can and then commit those moments to memory, to the memory of the heart. In the heart we ponder these memories until we pierce their surface and go directly to their essence. Thus these experiences, now memories, bring to birth a new depth of understanding and begin to create new patterns of human meaning, much like a weaving or a poem. In Rilke's words,

For the sake of a single verse, one must see many cities, men and things, one must know the animals, one must feel how the birds fly... And still it is not enough yet to have memories. One must be able to forget them when they are many and one must have the great patience to wait until they come again. For it is not yet the memories themselves. Not til they have turned to blood within us, to glance and gesture, nameless and no longer to be distinguished from ourselves—not til then can it happen that in a most rare hour the first word of a verse arises in their midst and goes forth from them. (Rilke, 1949)

3.

It is not fair to speak of Wisdom and the elderly in just the past tense, as if the elderly today are no longer wise. It is true that social structures and people's attitudes have, in the past hundred years, undergone a change the likes of which has never before been witnessed. Some of this is due to sheer numbers. By 1980, there were over 25.5 million people 65 years of age or older living in the United States alone, approximately 11.3 percent of the population. How many Wise Old Men and Wise Old Women can we have? Further changes have been wrought by the industrialization, specialization, and complexification of our society, as well as the breakup of the nuclear family. It is indeed difficult for Johnny to learn from grandpa's wisdom if Johnny lives in California and grandpa still keeps up the family homestead in Connecticut. And even if they do live within 20 miles, Johnny must still be brought to understand that grandpa and grandma just might have something worth hearing even if they can't "speak" it in Basic, Pascal or Machine Assembly Language.

Wisdom is not simply age, but it can be born of age. Wisdom is not simply fact, or a collection of facts, but it can grow from understanding these facts. Wisdom is not experiences, but it can be brought forth in Experience. Wisdom is something nurtured and tended in one's own soul. It is generated in a furnace fired by contemplation and insight. As Teilhard de Chardin wrote many years ago,

Thus, every man, in the course of his life...must build—starting with the most natural territory of his own self—a work, an opus, into which something enters from all the elements of the earth. *He makes his own soul* throughout his earthly days; and at the same time he collaborates in another work, in another opus, which infinitely transcends, while at the same time it narrowly determines, the perspectives of his individual achievement: the completing of the world. (de Chardin, 1958)

4.

Wisdom is alive today. When found it is like Grace, a gift freely given which enlightens and expands one's whole being. It flourishes perhaps like never before—not only in poems, books and memoirs—but also in the lives of hundreds and thousands of people. Wisdom is found not only in discourse, be it around a checkerboard in the park, a reminiscence group in a senior center or the dining room table. Wisdom can be found in the grace of a helping touch. Listen to these words of a 68 year old lady, a volunteer in a Foster Grandparent Program:

> What a surprise for me this year! This same little one now comes in the morning with a smile, struggling to remove his coat and eager to please. In spite of his physical handicaps which include a severe speech impediment, and also in spite of the fact that English is not spoken in his home, we are able to communicate through sign language and he is able to participate in group sessions and is showing a remarkable ability to learn. He is a bright, responsive and observing child and only needed some small encouragement to open the door to a new world for him.

Sometimes Wisdom is not altogether obvious. Sometimes it is hiding beneath the surface, and sometimes it is not yet distilled from the raw material of life's experiences, but it is there. For over a decade I have worked almost daily with the elderly. I have shared much of life's joys and especially its pains and sorrows, and I have come to learn much from these people whom I was supposed to help. It was like Grace, this Wisdom.

Sometimes it was freely given, lavishly bestowed. Sometimes it had to be mined, two of us sitting together in darkness until a light appeared. But it came. Each time it came.

This book is about the Wisdom I have witnessed in daily contact with these elderly people. I have included stories of many people, of their daily lives, their hopes and dreams as well as their setbacks and anguish. I share these because, "...I believe we learn through the experience of others as well as through our own, constantly meditating upon them, drawing the sustenance of human truth from them..." (Sarton, 1977) But this book is more than a collection of experiences or even Experience. I have processed these moments of shared life through the furnace of my own soul, and have added some color and spice from writings which I believe represents our collective Wisdom. Most of this book is presented as a series of "thoughts," in order to allow the reader ample opportunity to stop and turn inward, to begin or to add to his or her own seeking of Wisdom. Finally I have added some "exercises," each designed to facilitate an "experience" of the heart of the matter under discussion. It is my hope that the contents of this book will point us all in the direction of Wisdom.

2

Remembering

Old people and memories seem to go hand in hand. Old people tell stories, sometimes again and again. They tell us of the "good old days," when things were done "right." Some of the elderly seem to spend most of their days reminiscing. Remembering is an important part of aging, but not only of aging. Remembering is a part of almost everyone's life and, as we shall see, a crucial operation of the inner life, the psyche or soul, of each and every person.

1.

Last night the rains came in their typical Northern California way—cold and hardly more than a mist. The moon barely showed through the mist. As I left my office and walked towards my car I caught a passing smell, a hint of a redwood and the damp sandy soil in which it was planted. That smell took me back to a time of childhood, a time when I was six years old in the North Woods of Wisconsin. I remember playing in a wading pool. There were spots of intense sunlight shimmering on the water. I looked up to see the morning sun shining through the branches of a fir. It was a warm sun and the fir filled the air with its fragrance. Instantly, my memory zoomed into fast forward. From this special time of sunlight I remembered my interests in light—in painting and drawing, in photography, in French Impressionism, and my fascination with physics which opened me to Eastern philosophy. One passing fragrance and a pattern of life understood and highlighted in memory.

2.

Pre-printing-press societies normally gave remembering a special place. The elders of these societies held their societies' myths and rituals in their memory. These stories contained the basic identity of the group and each member of it. In remembering and retelling these stories, the elders recreated the history and identity of each member of that group and of the group as a whole. This occurred during rituals of initiation.

Homer's epic poem *The Iliad* presents an interesting example of the nature and power of remembering. In pre-Homeric days each city-state had tales of its own heroes. These tales contributed to civic pride and identity. Individuals could claim to be descendants of Ajax, Hector or another hero, thus establishing a sense of identity. As bards travelled from city to city, they retold tales of their host city, perhaps their own city of origin, and other tales learned along the way. Soon these were fused together into the epic which became known as *The Iliad*. A greater pan-Hellenic identity was being woven as the patterns of these stories took form in the remembering and the retelling of the bards. Tradition remembers Homer as an old blind man, seer not of externals but of inner truths. His rememberings created the patterns which carried and bestowed identity to a nation.

3.

When I was young I used to listen to my grandfather tell stories of the old country, Poland. He told of his father riding in a hay wagon with the local priest. He told of mountains and mountain folk, wild and lovable. He spoke of the earth and crops, of festivals and daily life, of his parents' wisdom and foibles. Poland came alive for me. It coursed in my blood. I was proud to be a Pole and proud to be one of the family.

When I went to school we studied the Polish language, culture and history. Somehow those studies never touched me. King Jan Boleslaw and all the others were in some hazy distant past. I never knew what they were like, who they were. But I knew of my great-great grandfather and the country priest; and I knew that on Christmas Eve we waited for the first evening star, just like my family always waited, just like all real Poles waited. I knew when we sang carols of Christmas or the lamentations of Lent that I was being a Pole. I knew because of grandpa's stories.

Grandpa taught me much more than what it was to be a Pole and to be a member of our family, though this is an inestimably valuable lesson. Grandpa taught me the creative power of the Word, the power by which Genesis presents God as creating the world, an understanding echoed in the opening words of the Gospel According to St. John, "In the beginning was the Word...." Remembering takes place by means of images embodied in words. In telling tales, grandpa was creating and recreating a reality in his imagination and mine. A powerful reality.

Last Christmas I remembered a story my grandfather was fond of telling. It seems that his grandfather, my great-great-grandfather, was a close confidant of the local parish priest. They were the only two people in town who could read. This priest once shared a book with my forebear after having sworn him to secrecy. It was a book of history and prophecy, foretelling marvels like great flying metal birds and disasters like world consuming wars. The priest felt it was beyond the scope of his average parishioners. My grandfather never saw this book, written by some

Frenchman, but he described much of it from the memory of his great-grandfather's stories. Last Christmas I remembered my grandfather's tale when I began to read one of my Christmas presents, *The Prophecies of Nostradamus*. Because of my grandfather's remembering, I now entered a new realm. Not only was I reading a new book, but I was also bringing to consciousness and completing a family task begun five generations before. Remembering.

4.

The Persian doctor Avicenna (Ibn Sina), whose eleventh century writing was the primary source of Aristotle for the Western world, wrote about *ta'wil*, spiritual exegesis. Henry Courbin has called *ta'wil* Avicenna's "most characteristic mental operation." (Courbin, 1980) In *ta'wil*, a person studies a text,

> "...recalling, returning to its origin, not only the text of a book but also the cosmic context in which the soul is imprisoned. The soul must free this context, and free itself from it, by transmuting it into symbols." (Courbin, 1980)

In this understanding the inner life of a person is in exile on this earth. The soul must remember the Divine place of its origin in order to attain salvation. This place is remembered by bringing alive a text, re-creating it in the imagination. Once this divine reality is present, the soul expresses itself in a symbol which carries this reality and moves the soul farther on its journey home. Thus remembering recreates the original reality. Perhaps this can be accomplished by using not only spiritual texts but moments of life as the starting point for the soul's *ta'wil*. A spiritual exegesis of life can thus be carried on by the imagination, resulting in the recreating of places in the inner life, and the creation of symbols as our way of accessing these "places." Thus the memory, by means of imagination, recreates life, transforming it into a psycho-spiritual experience, delineating an inner geography.

5.

Tony was 76 when I got to know him. He used to love to tell me stories of his family home, Modenna, Italy. He spoke of its famous sausages and cheeses. But most of all he loved to tell stories of operas staged at the Theatro Communale. This was the opera house that gave the world Luciano Pavarotti and Mirella Freni. Tony would relate the plots of these operas, elaborate on their settings, costumes, etc., and spice his stories with off key renditions of crucial arias. It took me months to realize that Tony had been born in New York and had never been out of the country.

Should we accuse this man of lying or of leading a delusional life to satisfy his ego's needs? Perhaps that is the case, but more than that is at stake. Albeit in a rather unsophisticated manner, Tony is performing an ex-exegesis of his own soul. For Tony, music is an approach to the Divine. Tony's inner life is filled with the beauty of music, the Divine Harmony. His stories of Modenna give him a grounding, a point of reference. Much like an Ancient Greek could claim to be a descendant of Hector or some other hero, this second generation Italian claims to be a son of Modenna, the locus which gave the world the beautiful music of Pavarotti, Freni, et. al. Tony is weaving a text, the story of his psychic life, which is the starting point for his soul's exegesis of itself. He does not, however, take it far enough. In Avicenna's understanding of *ta'wil* the soul is returned to its Divine Source. Tony's stories provide the soul with grounding but end at a rather personal level. Tony needs to "see through" this personal level to a transpersonal, archetypal realm. Perhaps Tony is not using enough imagination, i.e. it is not image-inal enough.

6.

'San Francisco' is a place-marker as much as for the memories we have of this city as for any more existential or pragmatic consequences it may have for our lives. *Place-heart-memory:* here is a genuine *mysterium conjunctionis* which yields heart as the place of memory, memory as the place where heart is, place as the memory

where heart is left, heart as what is left of remembered place....
(Casey, 1982)

Remembering moves the heart, the feelings; memories move the imagination; and imagination moves the soul. Remembering creates a place within the psyche in which a thing may dwell. Aristotle said that things exist insofar as they have space. Remembering creates space, many spaces, all living in relationship to each other. These spaces form patterns. Imagination can move these patterns around, shift them, sort and resort them to create new patterns, new textures. These patterns become the textures and texts of our lives. Remembering brings forth the texts of our lives, creates our stories, and brings us to life.

In other words, each of us has certain themes in our psychic life, themes which recur at periodic intervals as we move through life. Sometimes they may become most evident in the patterns of our feelings, for example a cycle of loneliness/isolation, then self-recrimination, then a feeling of being smothered, followed finally by a yearning for the Divine. Perhaps this cycle can be seen in a pattern of dream images. It may take days, months or even years for these cycles to come full swing, but they inexorably do. The psyche dwells in a cyclic pattern of mythological time. With each occurrence of one of these themes, as the patterns re-enter our feelings, actions, or images, they may become reference points to help us re-orient our inner lives, creating our inner maps. In watching for the slight variations in these themes we can gain an understanding of the movement and direction of the psyche's inner workings.

One of my clients experienced such an inner cycle in his dreams. For many months Bill recorded his dreams each morning. At first both of us felt lost, as if we were wandering in some deep dark wood of the psyche. There appeared to be no sense or direction to this man's life or his dreams. Slowly, however, a pattern began to emerge. First came images of clowns. Days, or sometimes weeks, later Nazi storm troopers appeared in his dreams. Finally seductive women would appear. These images would cycle back again and again, frequently with minor changes. The clowns would cry or be happy. The storm troopers would viciously attack or provide shelter and protection. The women would seduce, belittle or act as inspirational companions. Using these inner points of reference, Bill soon began to construct a geography of his soul, a road map of its heights, widths and depths. As he grew in skill, his inner life became a source of strength and guidance. He reminded me of Susan Sontag's description of Walter Benjamin, a contemporary philosopher, essayist and critic:

> His goal is to be a competent street-map reader who knows how to stray. And to locate himself, with imaginary maps. Elsewhere in *Berlin Chronicle* Benjamin relates that for years he had played with the idea of mapping his life. For this map, which he imagined as grey, he had devised a colorful system of signs that "clearly marked the houses of my friends and girl friends, the assembly halls of various collectives,...the hotel and brothel rooms that I knew for one night,..." He managed to draw a diagram of his life: it was like a labyrinth, in which each important relationship figures as an "entrance to the maze." (Sontag, 1981)

Bill, however, was not creating a street-map of actual locations. He was charting the patterns of inner images, images presented to him from the depths of his psyche. These images are archetypal images, i.e. manifestations of the archetypes playing within and through Bill's soul.

7.

Before you begin this exercise, please read the chapter of this book entitled, "Instructions for using the exercises found in this book." This exercise also requires that you do some drawing, so please gather some large sheets of paper, like a newsprint pad, and crayons or your favorite drawing medium.

Sit back, relax and let yourself take an adventure in your imagination. Let yourself be transported to a country. Not just any country, but one which has never been explored and charted. Imagine yourself placed in some specific spot in this country. Look around and get the general scope of the place. Is it an island? Is it landlocked? Mountainous? Desert? Green and fertile? Arid? Allow your imagination to roam and present you with as full and graphic a description as you are able. Don't forget the sounds, smells and textures. If you can't imagine in pictures, don't worry about it. Use words or thoughts or just feelings.

Now as you roam around this country, imagine that you stumble upon a place from your childhood. Maybe it will be the memory or an actual place encountered in childhood. Maybe it will be someplace that reminds you of a childhood place for one reason or another, or maybe you will find an image which you can use as a symbol of a childhood place. Spend some time with it. Let it develop and grow. Notice the sights and sounds, and all the memories associated with this place in your history. Allow this experience to form itself into some specific image, either a picture or some words which will be a symbol to remind you of this experience. Remember this symbol. Fix it carefully in your mind (or make a few notes on a piece of paper) and remember the location in which you discovered it.

Now pick a direction and begin to walk on. Soon you will come to another place from your past, this time from your teen years. Perhaps it will be associated with school, home or friends. Perhaps something else. Notice this place. Look around, let it become as real as possible. Pay attention to the memories which arise in relation to this place. Allow this experience to form itself into some specific image which will be a symbol to remind you of this experience. Remember this symbol. Fix it carefully in your mind (or make a few notes on a piece of paper) and remember the location in which you discovered it.

Continue walking in whatever direction you choose. Soon you will come upon yet another location, this time someplace related to your first love. Again let this place and all its memories reenter your being. Let this experience come alive. Recreate it. Allow this experience to form itself into some specific image which will be a symbol to remind you of this experience. Remember this symbol. Fix it carefully in your mind (or make a few notes on a piece of paper) and remember the location in which you discovered it.

Again continue your walk. Follow the same procedure you just did. Discover places connected with your marriage, your work, your parents, and any other significant moments in your life. Let your imagination and your soul suggest places for you. Maybe they'll be familiar, maybe not. Spend time in each one, allow each experience to form itself into a symbol, and mark its location.

Now gradually bring your awareness back to the room in which your body is located, back to your body, remembering the symbols of your experiences, and prepare for the second half of this exercise.

(Get out your drawing materials for the next part of this exercise.)

Choose your favorite pen, pencil, crayon, marker or whatever and draw a map-like outline of the "country" you have just visited. Find the location of the first spot you visited and at that location on the map draw the symbol which represents the experience you had there. Now continue to locate the places corresponding to the locations at which you had your "experiences," and draw their symbols on the map until you have included all of the places you have visited during this exercise. If you wish, at this point you can fill in your map with your country's geographic detail, e.g., forests, lakes, deserts, etc.

The country in which this exercise takes place isn't as important as are the locations you visit. You may begin your trip in your old neighborhood, hometown or wherever. Your journey is one of the imagination, a journey in which your imagination has taken the most important times of your life, created a psychic "space" for them, let you experience them as part of your inner being and begun to help you to interrelate them.

Spend a few moments noticing how these places relate to each other. Which are closest? Which farthest apart? Which ones are easy to get to, and which require arduous effort. Which places open in easy access to which other places, and which ones are only experienced in isolation. Look at the drawing of your symbols. Which have more "energy," (color, definition, emotional charge, feelings of attraction or avoidance)? Spend time ruminating about these areas of your inner life. Reenter them in your imagination, if you wish. Let them lead you on an adventure through your inner being.

You have begun to experience your own inner geography. With repeated effort you can easily begin to experience your inner life as a rich and interrelated world of intricate and shifting textures. These patterns may change. Understanding grows and deepens. Furthermore, as you repeat this experiment again and again, you will become aware that the images and patterns encountered in these visualizations begin to take on a life of their own. They are the work of the archetypes playing within your psyche, using the images of your life to weave their own pattern. Grounding your psyche in these patterns is akin to an exegesis of your own soul, a process which will lead the inner life to its own transpersonal foundation, and perhaps beyond.

8.

This way of mapping the inner life is a symbolic and imaginative activity which can have disastrous results if enacted in too literal a fashion. Consider the situation of Martha, an 83 year old woman.

Lost again.

It is difficult not to feel deeply moved at the sight of this lady, decked out in finery of a day gone by, wig slightly askew, lipstick lines awry, being brought home again by the local police. They all know her and treat her well, but the mixture of shame and bewilderment on Martha's face is telling.

Two or three times a day, every day, Martha goes for a walk. She seems to wander about without rhyme or reason, but she always passes through one of three locations—the garage where her auto is stored and the local branches of two banks. Most of the time Martha returns home safely. At times Martha gets lost, and that's when the local police enter the picture. Fortunately, they know her and like her. Martha gets lost when someone or something distracts her on her treck to the bank or garage, causing her to make a wrong turn or otherwise lose the narrow thread of her path. Twice this frail old lady has been mugged, fortunately without serious injury. Martha spends the remainder of her days thinking and worrying about her money and her auto.

The tendency to wander is frequently associated with senile dementia, and with the elderly in general. If they're not wandering physically, they're rambling in their stories and ruminations. They stalk the house, roam the halls of convalescent hospitals or just take to the streets. Treatment has run from locked attic rooms to locked hospital wards to prisons of chemical sedation. More current humanistic treatments include improving a person's reality testing and providing a safe and structured environment. Each of these treatments misses the important reality hidden in this behaviour, the need for a psychic, imaginal geography.

Martha returns again and again and again to the banks and garage. In her younger days, Martha married into an old and wealthy family. Her husband was good natured, loved her and loved life. They lived high and spent freely. Neither of them were great financial managers and by the time Martha's husband died there wasn't much left to the estate. Within three years Martha was reduced to poverty. Now, almost ten years later, Martha is driven to continual worry over her finances and her almost non-existent bank account balances.

Additionally, when Martha was young she loved her automobile. She and her husband set out on extensive motor trips at least once a month. They had even motored across the country twice, stopping in small towns, hob-nobbing with the locals, giving small town children rides in their shiny new sports car. Martha once likened her auto to an airplane. "I just flew through the streets, higher than a kite. Now I'm grounded. Trapped. Unfree." Grounded indeed. Though Martha's car was kept in a nearby garage, it had been decommissioned for her own safety. Six accidents in two months was just too much.

Martha's wandering is marked by several clear points central to her past life and focal to her present life. Martha wanders in the neighborhood in which she spent most of her life. Some days she passes the jeweler at which her fiance bought her engagement ring and at which they both later picked out wedding bands. Sometimes she stares into a dime store window, eyes fixed on the same soda fountain where she spent many a date. She walks past the dress shops at which outfits were purchased for each major event in her life, the drug store where she bought medicines which saved her children's lives, the baker who once sold her a cookie with a roach baked into it, etc. Martha physically re-enacts her own life-history in these seemingly random walks, weaving and re-weaving the patterns of the life on the streets on which it was lived; but this reenactment does not satisfy her and Martha is driven to repeat it day after day. It is too literal and material to be satisfying to the soul. In addition, Martha's family was very upset and worried about her physical well-being. They brought her in for therapy, hoping to "cure" her of her problem. Institutionalization was the only other alternative they could foresee.

Martha needed to "de-literalise" her behavior and restore it to its imaginative, soul nourishing qualities. Our first task was to discover the pattern which lay beneath her activity. This meant accompanying her on her walks and encouraging her to share her stories. While passing a dress shop, Martha spoke of her senior prom dress, bought from that merchant, and of the great time she had at the ball. At a jeweler she spoke of her husband nearly bursting with pride when he presented her with an engagement ring. At the dime store Martha spoke of sharing lunch with her grandchildren on summer walks. The meaning of Martha's wandering and the patterns of her life began to emerge.

The next step was to engage Martha's imagination. We began by working with her, constructing a small cardboard model of the area in which she would wander. Her granddaughter joined in this project. Then we encouraged her to "walk" a small plastic figure through this "city" and tell us her stories as the figure stopped at key locations. Martha enjoyed this activity and her stories fascinated us and her granddaughter. Martha repeated some stories and sequences almost verbatim, while she would modify others each time she retold them. She was beginning to create an imaginal geography, really a topography, of her inner life. She was weaving the text of her personal mythology. We next engaged the rest of Martha's family in her project. Soon they were working with her to write her autobiography and document the family's history. We also engaged Martha in a program of physical exercise to draw off some of the physical tension which her walking previously dissipated. Within two months, Martha's wandering had disappeared, replaced by a sophisticated act of the imagination. Her feelings of personal well being and self satisfaction attained a very high level.

9.

This need for an inner geography points to another archetypal dimension in which we all share. Since mythic time, or perhaps more accurately in mythic time, humanity has been envisioned as in exile. C.G. Jung, Mircea Eliade, Joseph Campbell and others frequently called myth the expression of humanity's deepest realities, shared both communally and individually. The myth of the Fall from Paradise is one of these central myths.

The Bible speaks of Adam and Eve's fall from grace and banishment from Paradise. An angel with a flaming sword prevents humanity's direct return to this idyllic state. Since then, humankind must wander the earth, living by toil and suffering travail. There is hope, however, of a return to grace by means of Redemption. In the Middle Ages the poet-philosopher Dante wrote one of the great masterworks of Western Literature—*The Divine Comedy*. This epic begins with the poet, a figure representing each and every person, lost in a dark wood. Mankind in exile. The individual person wandering without a sense of inner bearing. The poet is then guided, first by Virgil and then by Beatrice, through Hell, Purgatory and finally through Heaven to the throne of God. In this poem Dante drew a geography of the structure of the universe as it was then known and gave us a roadmap, using imagery from his worldview, for the soul's journey back to Paradise. (Luke, 1975)

We need not turn to religious disciplines to see the same need eloquently and powerfully presented. In *The Odyssey* Homer presents a mighty tale of Odysseus in exile, seeking above all homecoming. After the Trojan War Odysseus' ship was blown off course primarily because of Odysseus' inability to refrain from ego aggrandizing boasts. Odysseus was driven from adventure to adventure to the very center of Hades before he is finally reunited with his other half, Penelope, and his son and father. Ancient writers have used Odysseus' wanderings as an image of the human condition, namely, the divine soul, wandering in ignorance and delusion, trying to return home to its Divine Source as symbolized by homecoming and the Sacred Marriage. (Porphyry, 1969)

The images of wandering contain an important message for our lives. *The Divine Comedy* presents a kind of psychological-philosophical roadmap shared by a whole culture. *The Odyssey* presents an image of wandering seen as a spiritual quest of the inner life, the soul. The wandering old lady, Martha, by means of her personal pain, shows us our condition today—inner realities confused with outer manifestations, and no one collectively accepted roadmap. Each of us are adrift and each of us are faced with the task of confronting meaning and direction in our lives. There is hope, however, and guidance available in the depths of our beings, for each of us can begin to rediscover our own inner geography, our own inner maps composed of the images of our life and soul.

10.

Florida Scott-Maxwell, an octogenarian facing great physical infirmity and limitations wrote in a book based upon her personal journal,

> You need only claim the events of your life to make yourself yours. When you truly possess all you have been and done, which may take some time, you are fierce with reality. When at last age has assembled you together, will it not be easy to let it all go, lived, balanced, over? (Scott-Maxwell, 1968)

3

Silence

"I do so love to have the whole family over," she confided in me, "but I'm also relieved when they leave. All of those people with so much to say. So many words, some of them important for what they mean, some of them important because of who speaks them, but so much, well, *noise*. My head rings for days after they all leave. Sometimes I just am most happy being alone in this here house. It is so quiet, so peaceful."

These words were spoken by a 78 year old widow, a retired school teacher. They form an apt introduction to the subject matter of this chapter, the relationship between personal fulfillment, silence and retirement.

1.

Perhaps it was the radio, after all, that changed things. At least before radio a person could find a place where the only sounds to be heard were created by Nature, not that Nature didn't get raucous at times. But now, noise is everywhere.

Out on the river, paddling a canoe miles away from the nearest town, we seemed to take in the sights and smells by osmosis. We could hear the wind part the wild rice, even hear it make ripples on the water's surface. Then we heard *it*—the acid rock. The noise grew louder and louder. Its source took well over 10 minutes to reach us. My friend said that we should call it acid rain not acid rock. Finally a power boat zoomed by with two teenagers and their blaster. We almost capsized in its wake.

Radio may be a prime culprit but it is by no means the only source of noise pollution. Think of that quiet evening in the back yard, punctuated by the sounds of jetliners taking off and landing, or just flying by. Or the constant sounds of automobiles flooding the neighborhood with a backdrop of white noise. White noise—a product of our culture—a constant drone of unrecognizable sound used to drown out identifiable sounds. Some companies use white noise to "sound proof" their offices. Or then there are the landscapers' leaf blowers, or the television's babysitting an empty house or...

And then we can extend noise pollution to word pollution in general. Words jump out towards us, grabbing our attention and our minds. Billboards, signs in store windows, signs in other cars, signs everywhere, each shouting their must-be-heard message...

Max Picard has written,

> Everything begins and ends with noise. It does not seem to depend for its existence on man at all: it seems to be something objective outside him. The noise of words is not spoken by man at all: it is simply spoken all around him. It penetrates him, fills him up to the very brim, and the noise is what overflows through the edge of his mouth. (Picard, 1952)

Stimuli are everywhere, from every direction. At each moment something new is being presented, something which requires an emotional or intellectual reaction. But how many times can a person react in one day before the well runs dry, before the resources of thought and feeling are depleted? Either we are torn apart or we deaden our senses and our life. It used to be that a person could go off someplace to recharge, take some quiet time by oneself or with a close friend. Silence, a refuge. But today silence is "...no longer an autonomous world of its own; it is simply the place into which noise has not yet penetrated." (Picard, 1952)

2.

Aldous Huxley has written:

And this din goes far deeper, of course, than ear-drums. It penetrates the mind, filling it with a babel of distractions—new items, mutually irrelevant bits of information, blasts of corybantic or sentimental music, continually repeated doses of drama that bring no catharsis, but merely create a craving for daily or even hourly emotional enemas. And where, as in most countries, the broadcasting stations support themselves by selling time to advertisers, the noise is carried from the ears, through the realm of phantasy, knowledge and feeling to the ego's central core of wish and desire. Spoken or printed, broadcast over the ether or on woodpulp, all advertising copy has but one purpose—to prevent the will from ever achieving silence....Advertising is the organized effort to extend and intensify craving—to extend and intensify, that is to say, the workings of that force which (as all the saints and teachers of all the higher religions have always taught) is the principle cause of suffering and wrong-doing and the greatest obstacle between the human soul and its divine Ground. (Huxley, 1958)

3.

Frederica. 62 years old. Overweight in the stereotypical manner of a German *hausfrau*. She is alone since her husband died. Her friends worry about her but they can't seem to help. They feel her grief is going to speed her to her own death.

Frederica spends all day sitting in a worn out chair watching television. She is never without a television set turned on, and she has one in each of her rooms. Frequently all of them are turned on and, because of a mild hearing impairment, at substantial volume. They are usually not set to the same station. Her neighbors want to complain to the landlord, but they feel sorry for her.

When I first met Frederica, she would only discuss television programs. Game shows, entertainment specials, soap operas. She spoke of the characters as if they were real people, her friends and family. Her moods would change along with the fortunes of these people. I wondered why she needed to bury herself in all this noise. Was her grief so intense that she could not bear to be alone in silence?

There was one other peculiarity about Frederica. She spent almost all of her money on the books, records, gadgets, etc., advertised during the commercial breaks of her favorite soaps. She had a marvelous collection of off-label recording artists, but did not have a working record player. Often she bought records with her food money. At times she wrote bad checks because she wanted one of the products but was out of money.

It took some time for Frederica to open up and trust me, but when she did the grief she expressed was almost overwhelming. Soon she began to understand that the best memorial she could give her husband was to go on with her life as best as she could. She rejoined a club and began to volunteer at the childrens' ward of a community hospital. Frederica was an instant success with the kids because of her innate gift for storytelling and her huge repertoire of fairytales. She also began to reestablish old friendships and make new ones. At times she still misses her husband, they had lived a good life together, but she had found a new source of strength in herself and in her work. Frederica seldom watches the television. She says, "Oh, I don't have time for all of that now and besides, when I get home, I need time to myself. Time to think. Time to recharge for the next day." Nor does Frederica buy records, books and gadgets, about which she comments, "I don't know why I bought that stuff. I really felt I really needed it. But what I needed was here, in my own heart. I found that now."

4.

Diadochus of Photiki, a fifth century Egyptian Sage, said,

> When the door of the steambath is continually left open, the heat inside rapidly escapes through it; likewise the soul, in its desire to say many things, dissipates its remembrance of God through the door of speech, even though everything it says may be good. (Nouwen, 1981)

For a moment, let us consider this as a statement of *psychology*, the way the inner life works, and not of *theology*, the workings of God.

It is similar to the art of alchemy. In the popular imagination, the alchemists were at best slightly demented chemists trying to transform lead into gold. The popular imagination, however, misses the point. The alchemists were after what they called the *aurum non vulgum*, "the not common gold." They were seeking the "inner" gold, a deep transformation of their personalities and beings, and expressed this goal in the symbolism of their day. They performed experiments with matter and its transformations as an external image of what was happening within their psyche, as a kind of materially oriented meditation.

In the alchemical work, the experimentor would place a variety of materials into a vessel, seal it and apply heat. Heat and pressure would build within the vessel, thus effecting a transformation. Once the vessel would be opened, the heat and pressure would escape, thus aborting the experiment and eliminating the possibility of transformation. Keeping it closed too long and with too much heat could cause it to explode, also ruining the possibility of discovering the *aurum non vulgum*. The vessel used for the experiment became an image or symbol of the inner life of the alchemist. While it was sealed and cooking, the alchemist would silently sit and watch, meditating upon the transformations taking place in both vessels, the external apparatus of the experiment and his own soul.

In his autobiography, the Swiss psychologist C.G. Jung wrote that a person needs a secret to become a full individual. He illustrated this point with the story of how he had a childhood dream of the great Cathedral of Basl being destroyed by a giant turd dropped from heaven. Growing up in a strict and conservative Swiss Protestant family, he understood this dream to be highly blasphemous and would tell no one of it for fear of punishment. As a result it burned inside of him, making him acutely aware of the fact that he was different from the other members of his family and from his friends and companions. (Jung, 1963)

A person who has something burning inside, pushing to get out, blocked from escaping can become acutely aware of his or her inner life. Let the secret out and the pressure dissipates, along with that sense of inner life. This secret creates a sense of *interiority*, a sense of the reality and value of your inner life. Of course, the experience of interiority need not only come from traumatic incidents. The inner life is always present. However, opening the vessel too soon can damage the experiment. Keeping one's self in silence can be crucial.

5.

"I get up every morning at about a quarter past five. It's not that I can't sleep. It's just my favorite time of the day."

Fred is about 70 years old, but as he begins to speak about his morning walks he seems to visibly grow younger. Let us listen to the words of this retired factory worker whose parents carried him in their arms when they migrated from Italy.

"You know it's so different at five in the morning. No radios, no tv's, even the airplanes haven't started to fly. I get dressed and have some coffee, nice and warm on a cold morning, and walk to church. There's almost no one out, only the sound of a few cars going by with people who start work early. I walk a little over six blocks, but that is the high point of my day.

"As soon as I get outside I look up and look for Orion. My father didn't know much about the stars and things like that, but he taught me how to spot Orion. You know, he's the hunter. You can spot him by just looking for the three stars running down his sword belt. I can see him almost every day, unless there's clouds, taking his big walk through the skies. We're sort of alike you see. I take my walk down here, he's walking up there. We say hi to each other each morning, but we say it without words...

"I love it most in the winter. It's so quiet and when the ground is all covered with snow it's like walking in this world for the very first time. I know it's not right to say it, but sometimes I feel real close to God when I walk to Mass on winter mornings. I feel what he must have felt when he looked at the world for the very first time. Sometimes I feel closer to him on my walks than in church."

I asked, "Fred, do you ever feel like that at any other time or just when you go for your morning walks?"

"Well, sometimes when I'm in my garden I sort of feel close to that, but not really. During the day there's just too much noise. Oh, the neighbor kids are good kids, but they play their big radios, and you can hear tv's from next door, then there's cars and planes going by, then my wife wants to talk about something. Sometimes she just wants to talk. Now, none of that's so bad, but I can't feel close to God when there's all that noise. I need that peace and real quiet to feel close to God."

6.

(WARNING: The following is a very powerful exercise. If you are experiencing any form of mental or emotional illness or distress, please consult a licensed mental health professional before attempting the following exercise.)

The exercise is best performed with the help of a friend, although it can be modified for the use of only one person by following the directions before proceeding with the exercise.

Preparation: Obtain a pair of soundproof ear plugs from a local hardware or sports shop. (They are made of foam and are inexpensive.) Obtain a dozen 3" x 5" index cards. Label them from 1 to 11 and write the following information on each respective card. (You will have one extra card.)

Card Number	Information
1.	Your job title or a three or four word description of your work.
2.	The names of a few acquaintances.
3.	The name of a close friend.
4.	The name of another close friend.
5.	The name or a three or four word description of your favorite hobby or leisure time activity.
6.	Your parents' names.
7.	Your children's names, if you have children.
8.	Three of your favorite foods.
9.	Write the words, "your ability to speak."
10.	Your spouse or life companion's name, if you are in such a relationship, your closest friend's name if you do not have a spouse or life companion.

11.   Write the words, "your hearing."

Part One: Find a comfortable location at which you will not be disturbed for about an hour. Your friend should guide you through this exercise, reading or paraphrasing these directions in a slow and steady voice, allowing you to take your time with each step. At each of the following steps, try as much as possible to visualize the scene contained in these directions. If you do not "see pictures" at least use words or thoughts to carry out the directions. Also, it is *very important* to take a moment after each part of the following directions to notice whatever you are feeling. Try to keep this awareness in the back of your mind.

Hold the index cards you have prepared in your hands. Begin by spending a few moments relaxing and letting go of your daily concerns, schedules and expectations. Focus on your breathing. Without forcing yourself, take in deep and regular breaths. Imagine that with each breath you are taking in the relaxing warmth of the sun and allow it to circulate through your body, just as your blood circulates through your body. Let this warmth penetrate to any point in your body or mind where you feel any tension. Let it relax you deeper and deeper as it circulates throughout your body.

Now imagine that you are watching a kind of moving picture, the story of your life as you now are living it. Let yourself see pictures of your work, your acquaintances, friends, and loved ones, your hobbies and your daily life activities. Imagine now that this movie is a magic show and that you are no longer just a spectator but also a participant. Let yourself experience your life.

Now your friend will ask you to hold up your index cards. He or she will take the card numbered "1" and say to you, "Please imagine that you are no longer a _____. Imagine what your daily life is like without this work and everything which it brings to you."

After a few moments your friend will ask you to hold up your cards, take card number "2" and say, "Please imagine that _____ and

_____ are no longer a part of your life. Imagine what your life and your daily activities are like without them."

The pattern is to continue until you are left with only three cards. Your friend will ask to take away the next card, card number "9," saying, "Please imagine that you are no longer able to speak. Imagine whatever you have left in life but without the ability to speak one word to anyone. Imagine what's left of your daily life and its activities without speaking."

After a few moments your friend will ask you for another card and tell you, "Imagine that you have lost _____. Imagine day in and day out life without friends, family, without the ability to speak, and now without _____."

After another pause, your friend will ask you for your last card and hand you a set of ear plugs, saying, "Please insert these plugs into your ears. Imagine that you are losing your hearing. Picture your life without the ability to hear any sound at all. Remember to notice what you are feeling."

Part Two: After a while your friend will *very gently* tap you on your shoulders and ask you to remove the ear plugs. He or she will then continue:

Try to notice whatever you are now feeling and just let it be. Begin to focus one more time upon your breath. Imagine that you are still alone, but that you are now laying in a very peaceful and beautiful location, somewhere out in your favorite area of nature. Though it will be very still, peaceful and quiet, allow yourself to enjoy this natural haven.

Now please become aware of the fact that the sun is shining a warm beautiful sunshine. Feel the sun shine over your whole body, warming you, penetrating deeply within. Allow yourself to experience the warmth and support of the sun.

Now also become aware of the fact that this same sun is shining on everyone and everything on earth. Feel how it supports and nurtures you, and how it does this for every person on earth. Notice how it wraps you in sunlight and how it wraps everyone else. Notice, too, that it not only shines on this earth but throughout our solar system, filling not only you but all space with its energy and light.

After a few minutes, your friend will remind you of where you are and ask you to slowly bring your attention back into the room. Slowly become aware of where you are, stretch your muscles a bit, and rub your face with your hands. Spend a few moments comparing the feelings you experienced during Part I of this exercise with those you experienced during Part II.

Note: If you are not able to do this exercise with a friend, you can best facilitate your experience with the use of a tape recorder. Tape the instructions, speaking in a calm and steady voice. If you tape the instructions, you will not have to use the index cards, simply record the details as you speak. Allow at least three minutes between sets of directions to give yourself enough time to do the visualizations.

7.

In the Ancient Greek language, the word for "leisure" is *skole*. This became *schola* in Latin, which is the basis for our English word "school." For the Ancients, those people who gave us the foundations of our culture, knowledge had little to do with the possession of facts or power. It was a *theoria*, a type of "seeing" of reality, perhaps what we would call contemplation, accomplished in leisure. Aristotle believed that the reason we existed was to pursue this leisure time activity, knowledge and understanding, and that the reason we worked was to create the possibility of having leisure. In other words, the purpose of our life and work is to have leisure so that we can pursue knowledge, not as possession, but as contemplation. It seems that today we consider the purpose of our lives to be work.

There is much being written today on the subject of retirement. In fact, pre-retirement planning is being offered as a major field of concentration by "forward looking" universities. No doubt retirement is a crisis, a critical situation in life. No doubt, too, that many, many people have great difficulty dealing with this major life transition and its accompanying change of identity. No doubt that appropriate planning for retirement can ease the transition, but what is the hinge upon which all of this turns? It is what a person does with time, the newly found "leisure" of retirement. And the key to leisure is not activity but silence.

8.

Consider retirement as experienced by three different people.

Walter took over the family business when he was 40 years old. It was a neighborhood grocery and meat market. Under Walter's shrewd guidance the business grew. Two new locations in the first ten years, four more in the next ten and then a major shift in focus, no longer neighborhood markets but now suburban supermarkets. Walter is still Chairman of the Board, and now his sons are thinking of retirement. But Walter is more than Chairman of the Board. Walter is at the produce market at 4 a.m. haggling with his distributors. He involves himself in all of the contracts with meat suppliers. He spends his afternoons lecturing his sons and grandsons, managers of the family's supermarkets, on such things as product displays and mopping floors. Evenings are spent pouring over invoices and reports.

Actually all of the above should have been written in the past tense because 46 days short of his 69th birthday, Walter suffered a major stroke. His doctor had warned him of hypertension and an excessively driven lifestyle. Now his doctor had to refer him for counseling. Walter was having some difficulty adjusting to enforced retirement and partial paralysis. When I asked him why he kept himself so involved with the family business he answered that the business was the reason why his family stayed close to him. He never had time for his family and they never were close to each other. As long as he had his fingers in the pie they had to spend time with him. Retirement meant the loss of all his sources of self-esteem and support.

Then there is Yolande. Yolande is somewhere in her upper 60's. She won't give her exact age. She has six children, 11 grandchildren and one great-grandson, and she loves to spend time with all of them. But Yolande does other things too. She is on the advisory board of a neighborhood senior center, a volunteer visitor for a homebound seniors project and a board of director of a public service agency. The most amazing thing is the boundless energy she seems to exhibit. Yolande performs all of the work with a certain relaxed grace. One seldom finds her hassled and frantic. I asked her for her secret and she replied that if she could raise 6 children she could handle a few committees. Then she continued,

> My husband died almost five years ago. Before then I was a homebody, not that I wanted to be. He was, you know, macho, and he wouldn't let me do the things I wanted to. When he died I missed him. I still do. We loved each other very much. But I was not free. Now I'm doing what interests me whenever I want to do it. I only do what I want, when I want. I feel like I've just begun my life. But you know I spend time alone each day. Sometimes I pray. Sometimes I go out into my garden. Sometimes I just sit there quiet. I thank God for all he has given me and take time to be alone and enjoy it.

Then there is Louis, a man who took early retirement a few years back. Louis had worked running an assembly line machine all of his adult life. He was too tired to do anything but watch the television when he came home and didn't socialize too much except with some fellows from the local neighborhood pub. Early retirement looked like the dream of his life. No more getting up early. No more slaving at the sweat shop. No more taking orders.

A peaceful retirement it was, until the arguments began. Louis moped around the house all day. He started to get in his wife's way. They argued. Louis also began to be depressed. He didn't know what to do with himself. Things just didn't feel right and he didn't know why. He started to watch more and more tv. When he wasn't watching the television he was listening to the radio. The little transistorized box was becoming his constant companion. Louis stopped going to church, a radical move for a staunch Catholic of his generation. When his parish priest pinned him down, Louis apologized and said that he didn't go to church because there was so much slow time, quiet time. He just found it too difficult to sit in such quiet for so long a time. At 62 years of age Louis began weekly therapy sessions.

The man who couldn't let go of work, the man who couldn't face himself in silence, the woman who found new life in her later years. Individual people. Representatives of what seems to be the three most common reactions to aging.

9.

In spite of the fact that our society's technology has created a great array of labor saving devices, and its social structures have extended leisure time to virtually all its citizens, we are still plagued by a level of activity hard to describe as anything but frenetic. Time management seminars, stress and burnout seminars, counseling for families who have no time to talk with each other—these are among the hallmarks of our new world of labor saving devices.

Perhaps, as Huxley has suggested, advertising is responsible for raising our desires to possess something and everything; and day in and day out activity is the means by which we attempt to satisfy this greed. In this frame of mind, everything becomes both a possession as well as an instrument for greater acquisition. Knowledge becomes the possession of facts which leads to the possession of power which leads to mastery over people and nature. Love becomes the possession of the loved one which leads to the possession of pleasure and fulfillment. Is this not an endless chain of greed? Is this not the ego, that little sense of self, cut off from its grounding and support in a reality greater than itself, holding on for dear life? What happens to a person when faced with mounting desires, coupled with less buying power and decreasing outlets of activity? In other words, what happens to a person who faces retirement and life well into its seventh and eighth decades?

It can, indeed, be difficult for a retired person to feel a high degree of self-worth in a society based upon greed, acquiring possessions, noise and frenetic activity, especially if that person has no way to recharge him or herself from the inside. No one would deny the importance of financial security, a network of friends and loved ones and the importance of some productive work, but a sense of the inner self, of interiority, seems to be the most powerful antidote for the potential ills of retirement. Indeed, learning to be comfortable in silence may be the unspoken key to a successful and happy retirement.

10.

Silence, the antithesis of our society. Silence, not as the mere absence of noise, but as a powerful force in its own right. Silence, not only an abstention from noise but also an abstention from that whirl of activity which keeps our hearts and minds so occupied that we do not have to face the mystery present in every moment of our lives, not to mention our lives themselves. Sometimes we can learn this lesson in an easy way, but sometimes it takes pain to bring us to our senses.

At 62 Bill was a marvelous picture of a vigorous, energetic elderly gentleman. Married for the third time, there was still excitement and romance in his life, and even a bit of womanizing on the side. Bill was married three times because each of his previous wives became too dependent on him and were "dragging him down." He had five children and three grandchildren, whom he was looking forward to take camping at his first leisure opportunity. Recently retired, Bill was beginning to make one of his hobbies into a profitable business. He worked long hours and inspired those around him to do the same. Almost everyone who knew Bill marveled at his dynamism, energy and creativity. He seemed to have but one flaw—impatience. Always on the go at breakneck speed, he became very frustrated when something or someone got in his way, and he became quite exasperated with people slower than himself, including his wives, children and grandchildren. Then came a major coronary. Bill's life ground to a stop. After a long stay in the hospital, Bill confided,

> I almost died. I never thought life was so fragile. I looked at my hands—they were wrinkled. My feet looked old. I couldn't run as before, or be as sexual. I'm an old man—worse than dead—de-

pendent. I couldn't even wipe myself. Then it hit me. I was so embarrassed because I was dependent and because I was always so harsh to people who were weaker than I was. But life means more than that. For some reason, I don't know, I haven't been to church for decades, but I thought of Jesus on the cross, pinned down. He couldn't even get a drink if that soldier didn't give him one. I began to see that there was a whole lot more in life that I was missing—kindness, charity, love.

As we spoke, Bill told me how he had given up on religion, but that he was now beginning to understand how everything in this life is a gift and how it continually depended upon the grace of the giver to keep it going. Bill began to change his life, slowly and not without some difficulty. He began to take some vacations and camping trips, to spend time with his family and friends. Bill even began to play, something he had not done since his childhood. Bill was beginning to experience his retirement as leisure, and to escape from the tyranny of noise into the luxury of silence. It filled him with a great joy.

11.

In 1959 Archibald MacLeish received the Pulitzer Prize for his modern day setting of the story of Job, *J.B.* In it the Job figure, J.B., is presented as a Captain of Industry, a Wheeler- Dealer who was reduced to ashes, losing his business, home, children and nearly his wife. Though J.B. is rich in more profound overtones, perhaps it would not be too far from wrong if we used J.B. as an image of a person facing retirement, feared so often in our society as the gradual and inevitable loss of everything. If we permit this reflection, then the final words of the original script can summarize the value of silence and its offer of hope.

J.B. is speaking to his wife, Sarah. Organized religion offered them no satisfying help, so J.B. appealed directly to God. He explains to Sarah what he learned:

We can never *know*.
He answered me like the stillness of a star
That silences us asking.

No, Sarah, no:
We are and that is all our answer.
We are and what we are can suffer.
But...
        what suffers loves.

And love
Will live its suffering again,
Risk its own defeat again,
Endure the loss of everything again
And yet again and yet again
In doubt, in dread, in ignorance, unanswered,
Over and over, with the dark before,
The dark behind it...and still live...still love.
(MacLeish, 1958)*

4.

Believing

1.

Young men who see visions and old men who dream dreams. Our Western imagination has long associated these images with religious experience, but seldom have we taken their meaning seriously. Seeing visions usually makes us at least a little uncomfortable. And yet visions, or a new kind of seeing, are central to practically all religious traditions. Perhaps examining the experiences of some elderly men and women can help us to understand more of our selves and the "religious" aspects of our natures.

2.

An elderly lady has a vision in which she sees her God, a vision which fills her with peace. No matter how sure she is of her vision, communicating it to others may be hazardous, for it may engender discomfort and doubt, even in representatives of organized religions.

Annette was referred for evaluation by a Catholic priest who feared that one of his parishioners was suffering from a mental breakdown. Annette had been a daily communicant for most of her life, though she was now bed-confined, dying of cancer. Her priest was now bringing her communion twice a month. He was a young priest, a recent graduate of a liberal seminary, and he had many doubts about "mystical experiences." He feared that Annette was losing touch with reality.

When I arrived at her home, I first spoke with her daughter-in- law. She spoke of Annette as a gentle and loving woman, a person who presented few, if any, problems in being cared for. I first saw Annette sitting on her bed, eyes closed, fingering her rosary beads. When she realized I was in the room, she became very warm and open, speaking freely of her past, her present illness and pain, and her gratitude to her son, her daughter-in-law and her parish priest. At times she smiled, at times she grew sober, all appropriately matched to the content of her speech. When we came to discuss how she was feeling, the conversation went something like this:

"Annette, with all of your suffering and pain, and with the end apparently so close, how is it that you are so peaceful?"

"The priest, he brings me communion every two weeks. It feeds me, keeps me going. When he brings me communion I'm in heaven. I can hear the angels and see them around God's throne. One of them picks me up and gently flies me straight to Jesus. Sometimes it seems to last forever. The music is so beautiful. Just like in heaven."

"Do you actually see and hear these things?"

"Not with my eyes and ears, but with my mind and heart. You know, I've had a very hard life, but I tried to live by God's laws. I loved my family first and then I tried to love everybody. I suffered most of my life and now I'm close to death. But I know that an angel will take me home to that beautiful place, and everything I went through will be worth it. And you know, now everything and everyone reminds me of heaven. The sunshine reminds me of God's grace, the white linen and curtains of the peace of heaven, and the priest, he brings me Jesus. I'm waiting for my guardian angel to take me to Him."

It was almost immediately obvious that the priest's concern, though well intentioned, had no factual basis. Annette, stricken with the continuous pain of a cancer eating away her body, and refusing all mind-altering medication, was painfully aware of reality. It was also apparent that her religious faith had led her to the point at which she was experiencing profound mystical visions. In psychological terms, she had learned to break through the narrow confines of a too literal perception of material reality and the grip of ego consciousness. She had learned to see the world as transparent to the Spirit of Being, a metaphor leading her further and further into the deepest mysteries of Reality.

3.

Throughout history, religion, irrespective of its unique and specific manifestations, has filled one of two functions. For some people religion has provided a refuge. Religious beliefs and rituals provided comfort, support, and security. Little does it matter if the "enemy" be Satan, a warring tribe or the forces of nature, religion, by providing a direct connection to the Divine, helped make life in the world, this vale of tears, a bit more bearable.

But for others, religion has gone beyond the level of refuge into a realm of transformation. The metaphors enlisted to explain this somewhat elusive goal of transformation are numerous. They include mystical experience, metanoia (in which the quotidian mind is replaced by the Divine Mind) images of new birth or emergence into a new world, awakening, enlightenment, and on and on. All of these metaphors point in one direction. Somehow that aspect of a person which makes a person his or her most uniquely personal (the "form" of the person in the sense given to us by Greek philosophy) is changed, "trans-form-ation." This is not merely cosmetic surgery, but a total change of how that individual perceives and understands him or herself and the universe.

How this happens, and in fact what actually happens, is not fully accessible to the rational mind. Religious experience has as its object the Divine, the Wholly Other. As such we can never fully grasp the totality of the Divine, at least not with our limited consciousness. Rational discourse comes from and returns to this limited consciousness, and therefore is not an appropriate vehicle for religious understanding, which is more properly situated in the realm of mysticism and spoken of in symbols and images.

Symbols, when understood from the perspective of depth psychology, are not mere pictures. Carl Jung spent most of his professional life studying and writing about symbols and their role in the transformation process. He defined a symbol as the best possible expression for a reality which cannot be fully described. The symbol already contains the reality it points to, and it helps bridge the gap between what a person "knows" without the symbol and the very reality the symbol attempts to convey. For example, one morning Stella and Edward came to my office very upset. They had been married for almost 40 years, a very happy marriage, and now they found themselves locked in a never ending argument from which they could find no escape. Stella had lost her wedding band. During the counseling session both of them told me what that golden ring has come to mean to them. They reviewed a mutually clumsy first sexual encounter, the births of children, support during hard times, in other words, a life of growth from awkward but hopeful teenagers to mature and still hope filled adults. Somehow that symbol, that very ring, not only pointed to these powerful life experiences, but also contained them as its essential being.

The power of religious symbols is similar to the power of Stella and Edward's rings. These symbols do not simply convey a new set of information as would, say, a formula from nuclear physics. These symbols contain and convey a Reality. When experienced by the receptive mind, these symbols convey that reality, move consciousness from one level to another, begin to affect a powerful transformation.

4.

At 86 years old, Denise is still an active participant in various neighborhood and church sponsored organizations. She is greatly loved by most of the people in these organizations, and called "special" by these people, no doubt because of her vibrant, happy and gentle personality.

Denise came to America at the age of seven and was orphaned by nine. She grew up in a coal mining town where money and resources were scarce. Her first husband was an alcoholic who beat her. He left her a widow at 27, with three children and no income or savings. She scrapped out a living, suffering not only material hardship but also the deaths of two of her children. At 29 she married again, this time to a good man, but poverty continued to plague them and their three new children. Another son was killed during the war. When she was 68 years old, her husband died of a massive coronary. As Denise described these events, there was no bitterness in her voice. When asked how she could survive such a difficult life without having her soul filled with rancor, she replied:

> I do not know why God gave me such a hard life. At least he gave me one good husband and good children, even if he did take three of them away from me when they were still so young. God doesn't tell you why, you just have to trust him. But you know, life isn't always what it seems like. The whole world suffers. Many of my freinds were Jews who were beaten and tortured. Their families were murdered. But why all this suffering? For as long as I could remember I've prayed one whole rosary each day to the Blessed Mother of Czestochowa. Each and every day I always light a candle before her picture. When times were rough, that's when I felt her the closest. She gave me strength and guidance. Now she's like an old friend. She helps me see that suffering is just a part of the world and that I'm not any better or worse off than the Rocke-

efellers. Oh sure, they've got money, but life isn't money. But something else happened, too. It's so hard to find the words for it. I used to be angry, real bitter. And I had a terrible temper. I was even angry at God, but I think I took it out on the kids and the neighbors. But somehow that's changed, too. I used to always feel gyped, like I never got what was owed me. Now I know my place in life, and I also know the miracles and love going on all round me. I wish I could put it in words better for you, but I just can't find the right words for it. You pray to the Blessed Mother and she'll show it to you, too. I know.

Over the next few days, Denise explained in greater detail how her personality had changed. As a young woman she suffered from a very negative self-image and experienced very critical self-judgements. These negative judgements were so all pervasive that she believed them to be a normal part of life, the way it was for everyone. Most of the time she wasn't even aware of them, and most of the time she was driven to extreme intolerance and criticism of just about everyone. She expressed her belief that her critical nature played a significant part in her first husband's turning to alcohol. The picture of herself she described was diametrically opposed to the one she presented in her current daily life, yet from all indications it was an accurate picture. When I spoke with her, Denise was neither overly self-critical nor a compulsive "do-gooder." Her devotion to the Virgin of Czestochowa had indeed brought about a major transformation of her personality. What powers lie hidden in this image and these rituals?

5.

Devotion to the Black Madonna of Czestochowa was crucial to Denise's sense of well being. That cannot be denied. Denise had experienced a profound transformation of her consciousness by means of her devotion to this religious figure. What created or facilitated this transformation?

The Black Madonna of Czestochowa, located at the monastery of Jasna Gora ("The Bright Mountain") in Poland is one of the most famous of about a dozen Black Madonnas. Some other well known Black Madonnas are in Einsiedeln, Switzerland; Montserrat, Spain; and Guadalupe, Mexico. Though each of these Virgins has a large cult, and each of them has a distinct image and legends, they all share some common traits. All of these Virgins are called Black Madonnas because their images are darkened. Non-Christian religions also have Black Madonnas, for instance, Kali, the Hindu goddess of death, destruction and resurrection; the Egyptian goddess Isis; the Greco-Roman many breasted Artemis; and Old Spider Woman of the American Indians. Psychologically, all of these images relate to a major underlying myth, the Great Earth Mother. (Gustafson, 1976) These Virgins and Goddesses may be seen as Earth Mothers, destructive and yet life giving, protectors of the life cycles, darkly instinctive and mysteriously potent.

The Black Madonna of Czestochowa psychologically participates in this realm. She is a mother carrying her son, the infant Jesus. She is the birthplace of the New Spirit. Yet she is also a virgin, a symbol of the untouched psyche, source of all psychic possibilities. She is black and is venerated by the peasants of the earth. Legend holds that this icon was blackened when thrown into a blazing barn by barbarian invaders. Miraculously, the image remained intact. Psychologically this represents the casting out of feminine consciousness by an overly aggressive masculine consciousness. The Black Madonna of Czestochowa thus mediates the outcast dark elements of the feminine principle, the earthy, bodily, instinctive, intuitional realms. She is wounded, carrying two Hussite scars on her cheek. Furthermore, she is a healing image, said to have been painted by St. Luke the Evangelist, himself a physician. In other words, she also represents the healing power of our wounds and the power of symbolic images to heal us, for symbolic images lead us back to those dark and outcast parts of our souls, leading us to wholeness. Though the images of the Black Madonna of Czestochowa are concrete, it is important to realize that they are never taken on a literalized, material level. Mary is never worshipped in her own right. She is venerated as the Mother of God. That she is seen as an archetypal, transpersonal reality is indicated by the fact that her image is enthroned and surrounded by a golden halo. She is regal, i.e. archetypal. Furthermore, in this religious symbolism, she is called the

Moon in relationship to Christ, the Sun. Thus, while she represents the earth Goddess, the dark, feminine side of the Godhead, she is venerated only in so far as she points to Ultimate Reality. In other words, her reality is that of a symbol, of metaphor, whereby body, instinct, emotion and intuition become transparent, leading each person deeper and deeper into conscious contact with the Ultimate.

What does all this have to do with daily life as we live it? Let us once again consider Denise's experience. Denise transformed the raw material of her life by means of her devotion to the Black Madonna of Czestochowa. Neediness opened her soul and through ritual faithfully repeated and through contemplation performed with all the powers of her heart, mind and soul, Denise learned to let go of the illusions that her ego is the center of the universe and that the material world is the goal and meaning of life. She learned how to see through the ten-thousand manifestations of reality to its essential core, and to see all reality as a metaphorical enactment, a player's mask as it were, of the Divine. The empowerment for these insights and accompanying transformations of her personality came not from her ego and its narrow consciousness, but from transpersonal symbolic images of the Divine, and, ultimately, from a Realm Beyond.

6.

Not all visions are health giving. Not all visions are the result of profound religious conversions. Who would give credence to a paranoid schizophrenic claiming he was told by God to exterminate all of the people of his neighborhood because they were sinners? But sometimes it is much more difficult to judge the meaning of a vision. Consider these three women.

Bertha is an isolated 71 year old lady, nearly blind, suffering from the later stages of Parkinson's disease. Many a day she cannot hold a spoon steady enough to feed herself. She refuses help from practically everyone, claiming to have no need of help because she is living on a different plane of being. Contact with lower planes is not only unnecessary but also polluting. She also claims that people want to have power, a power which she now has, but they aren't ready for it, so she has to protect them. If they come into contact with her and her power they may accidentally come into a very dangerous situation.

Marge is 91 years old. Her parish priest referred her to a counselor after she came to him to beg him to intercede for her with God because God was punishing her by making her live too long. When asked how she knew that God was punishing her she replied, "Because God told me so." Her priest wondered if she were not morbidly depressed.

Mary is an elderly lady who prays about four hours each day in a very traditional manner. Whenever she speaks to people she claims that she sees Jesus' face and she usually talks to them about love. She gives away practically all of her money to people who live on the streets, and she often invites them to come and stay at her "place."

Which of these ladies is mentally ill and which of them is experiencing profound religious transformation?

7.

Profound religious experiences can cause serious turmoil to the person experiencing them as well as to those who care for him or her. This is especially true if someone has a mystical experience and is not under the direct guidance of a spiritual guide. And yet these experiences are very common. They change how one perceives him or herself, and how one understands the world he or she lives in. They even change how a person actually perceives reality, and that could create some serious emotional and psychosomatic conflicts. It is indeed crucial to be able to make a distinction between psychotic and mystical experience. One would not want to perform the disservice of not obtaining appropriate care for a florid psychotic, nor would one wish to relegate a genuine mystic to some asylum's back ward or a half-way house. Traditional psychology, primarily because of its medical model and materialistic bias, offers little assitance in this task of discriminating between alternate states of consciousness. Transpersonal psychology, in the shadows of James, Jung, Maslow, et al., offers more significant guidance.

Christina and Stan Grof have pioneered research in the area of spiritual states of consciousness and have labelled these experiences "spiritual emergence." In essence they define a spiritual emergence as...

> (spiritual emergence experiences are...) Episodes of unusual experiences that involve changes in consciousness and in perceptual, emotional, cognitive, and psychosomatic functioning, in which there is a significant transpersonal emphasis in the process, such as dramatic death and (re)birth sequences, mythological and archetypal phenomena, past incarnation memories, out of the body experiences, incidences of synchronicities (Kundalini awakening), states of mystical union, identification with cosmic awareness....

Occasionally these spiritual experiences are accompanied by strange body sensations, such as energy, light or heat streaming through the body. Visionary experiences of both images and sound are common, as is temporary mental disorientation. Some people experience newly found psychic powers. They are discovering that these states of consciousness are more frequent than anyone has previously imagined.

The Grofs have proposed criteria for assessing an experience as a "spiritual emergence." An organic brain disorder must be ruled out, as must physical disease which would produce secondary alterations of a person's mental state. I would add that especially in working with the elderly, diet and blood chemistry must be carefully examined. Furthermore, the subject must be free from a long history of psychiatric disorder and treatment, and must be physically healthy enough to endure the frequently strenuous psychological work needed to integrate his or her new perceptions, understandings, etc. The remaining criteria are as follows:

> The ability to see the condition as an inner psychological process and approach it in an internalized way; the capacity to form an adequate working relationship and maintain the spirit of cooperation. These criteria exclude people with severe paranoid states, persecutory delusions and hallucinations, and those who consistently use the mechanisms of projection, exteriorization and acting out. (Grof and Grof, 1978)

8.

The insights presented by Stan and Christina Grof are extremely valuable, especially for counselors or clinicians attempting to diagnose a particular situation. Even at that, however, they deal with large, "big picture" features. Frequently mystical experiences are more "quiet," and people experiencing them maintain a high level of activity and daily life coping. Are there additional guidelines which we can use to help our understanding of these situations? Perhaps we can look to mainline Western Christianity for some insights.

Western Christianity has a rich tradition of mystical experiences. In these experiences people are "taken out of themselves." These experiences are frequently so ineffable that they are expressed only in poetry and allusion. People experiencing these experiences frequently have great difficulty understanding them and integrating them with the business of daily life. Traditions of spiritual direction have been developed to assist these "spiritual pioneers." In order to assist the spiritual directors in their highly individualized art, traditions have been established to provide general guidelines to ascertain whether the experience is from and reverts to a Divine Source or a Diabolical Source. This form of spiritual direction is called the "discernment of spirits." These guidelines are psychologically very astute, so much so that they may provide a valuable adjunct to our standard diagnostic criteria. In order to do so, we need to change "Divine Source" to healthy or normal and "Diabolic Source" to pathological. This is an operational change involving no philosophical positions.

Mystics traditionally stress that the first result of "transpersonal" experience is an increase in love. The person who is drawn into deeper and deeper knowledge of the Divine becomes both at peace with self and at the same time thirsting for greater communion with the Ultimate. The Divinity is characterized by Love, and this love spills out onto the subject and his or her actions. If the experience is a genuine transpersonal or mystical experience, the subject will not seek to control those around him, even by very subtle means of manipulation. Rather, tolerance and compassion result from a transpersonal experience of the Divine. The subject may feel sorrow at the wrongdoings of another, but there will be no attempt to force a conversion. One of the most important results of a mystical experience is a deep peacefulness. This peacefulness is normally not shouted in the streets, but cherished in a very quiet and personal manner. A sense of inner peace and "rightness" predominates.

Actions which point to the fact that an experience comes from the forces of evil or destruction, i.e. that may be seen as pathological or destructive to the personality, include: a claim to know the specifics of absolute truth, stunted awareness or growth, judgementalism and strongly critical attitudes, schismatic and divisive thinking, dependency, perfectionism, and enjoyment of suffering for its own sake, chronic depression and shunning joy. In these cases, the experience is to be treated as if it were destructive to the person having the experience. It is important, however, to remember that the subject must be treated not judgmentally but with great compassion. This does not rule out appropriate limit setting or loving confrontation, but it is important to remember that only genuine compassion can help the person turn towards health and healing. (Kelsey, 1978)

9.

Let us return to Mary, Bertha and Marge, the three women we have met earlier and see whether these newly found criteria can help us to better understand their experiences.

Mary, the elderly lady who gives away all of her possessions and sees Jesus' face in the people she meets, has no history of psychiatric disorder, but she does claim that her vision comes from God, not herself. Her experiences have significant transpersonal content. On psychological grounds alone, we may be left with an inclination to call her experience "healthy," but perhaps a bit of doubt still exists. However, when we introduce the criteria of discernment, the picture comes into very clear focus. Everyone who knows Mary realizes that her experiences are powerful sources of strength, peace, creativity and charity. She is filled with an inner peace and is a source of inspiration to many. In fact, the description of "Mary" is really a self-description of the Nobel Laureate Mother Theresa of Calcutta.

The case of Bertha, the lady with Parkinson's disease who is living on a different plane of reality, is less obvious and requires careful attention. Though she has no history of mental disorder, Bertha's vision seems to be a denial of reality, rather than an enhancement of it or a vision of its deeper dimensions, and her actions seem to be rather self-destructive. Yet a very important fact about Bertha is that she always seems to be content and at peace with herself. Nor does she attempt to use her powers in any form of self-aggrandizement. In fact she has great compassion for those who do not "understand" and consequently could be harmed by these powers. The truth of the matter is that her experiences are extremely powerful and very positive, and she is more than willing to enter into a dialogue with anyone whom she thinks understands these mysteries. Part of the problem is that "levels of reality" and "spiritual/psychic powers" are frequent features of most religious systems. However they are usually understood as "religious" or "psychological," and not "material" or "concrete" realities. In other words, they are seen as spiritual or metaphorical realities. Bertha, however, sees them as literal and not metaphorical. She needs to learn how to differentiate "levels of reality" and how to "integrate" them into her life and the life of the World. A *prima facie* understanding would have labelled Bertha as seriously pathological, a label which would have driven her further into the isolated world of her misunderstanding.

Marge, the 91 year old lady wishing to die, presents the other side of the story, for her experiences point to a debilitating pathology from both a traditional diagnostic point of view as well as from the point of view of the discernment of spirits. Marge's call from God was not a genuine transpersonal experience, a call to the life of the spirit, for it cut her off from life, enwrapped her in a world of isolation and bitterness and sealed her in a cloak of depression. In point of fact, a change in residence and the development in her life of a close personal relationship brought about an almost complete reversal of her symptoms with a subsequent enlivening of her personality. Marge's experience of Divine punishment was Old Man Depression masquerading as a religious experience and criteria from the discernment of spirits, confirmed by the insights of transpersonal psychology helped to confirm a positive identification of the culprit.

10.

Find a comfortable and quiet location and set aside the next forty-five minutes. Sit with your back straight but not held rigidly, and begin to breathe slow and regular breaths. Let yourself become one with your breath. Now slowly notice any tension in your body and let go of those spots. Imagine that you are able to direct your breath to these tense spots and the warm, regular breath gently massages all the tightness away, carrying it out of your body the next time you let your breath flow out.

Now imagine that you are in front of an elevator. Look carefully at the door. You are the only person there. Notice that inside the elevator is a plush and inviting chair. Step into the elevator and sit in the chair. Let yourself sink into this plush chair. Enjoy the relaxing feeling that comes over your whole body as you sit in this chair. Notice the doors begin to close and see above the doors a half-circle dial with a big arrow indicating the floor you are on. You notice that the elevator is now on the 10th floor.

Slowly the elevator begins to move downward. Let yourself sink into the chair and watch the dial slowly move. As you pass the 9th floor, let yourself sink deeper into your chair. Notice any tension you may have in your body and let it go. Let it be replaced by a deeper and deeper sense of relaxation and well being, a deeper relaxation with each lower floor. You pass the 8th floor. More relaxed. The 7th floor. You notice your body is feeling heavier, your mind more relaxed. Any tension spots you notice seem to dissolve away. As you pass the 6th floor you feel a deep sense of well being, knowing that all of your cares will be taken care of. You feel perfectly at ease, and let go of all your tension. The 5th floor leaves you more relaxed, as does the 4th floor. Let yourself feel very heavy. As you approach the 3rd floor you wonder how much more relaxed you can get, and you enjoy the warm relaxing feelings even more. At the second floor you notice just a little bit more tension and tightness in your body, just the hint of some concern passes your mind and you allow it all to dissolve away. You feel heavy, relaxed and a perfect sense of well being. As the elevator approaches the 1st floor you let yourself experience a deep sense of security. You do not know what you will experience in the next few minutes, but deep down you are confident that it is right for you to be here and that whatever you will experience will be a great benefit for your well-being. You let yourself go.

You notice that gradually the lights in the room begin to dim. Bit by bit the room gets darker, but your eyes become accustomed to the darkness and you can see in the dark as clearly as if it were the day itself. You notice that the room begins to shrink in size. There is no feeling of fear, just a great curiosity. It seems as if you are shrinking along with the room. Soon the room is tiny, and very dark. You feel very cozy and very protected.

You see a small opening on the other side of this room, just big enough for you to crawl through. You begin to crawl through this opening, like a tunnel, and it gets smaller and smaller. You have no fear and you know you must go through this tunnel, even though it gets more and more confining, more and more tight. Just when you think you can't push through any further, it opens up.

You find yourself floating in space. It is a beautiful, free float. You gaze around and see the stars, millions of them, the constellations and nebulas, the planets. Now notice that you are floating in a certain direction. In the distance you begin to see your destination. You see a perfectly formed man made of pure gold. He is shining like a sun, but the light does not hurt your eyes. In fact, it warms your whole body. The man is standing in front of a *typical scene from your life*. Spend a few moments and watch the scene. Note all of the details as faithfully as if they were happening at this very moment...

Observe as this golden man steps toward the scene and reaches for what looks like a curtain. As he moves the curtain aside, you realize that this episode of your life was only the decoration on the curtain. As this scene is moved aside, you realize that it is as if it had no reality of its own. In front of you is simply a nature scene, flowers, grass, water, trees, clouds and lots of different animals. Spend some time enjoying the view...

Now the golden man pulls aside another curtain and you realize that the world you thought you were seeing was nothing more than another curtain, and you are left in space facing this golden man and the vastness of space itself... Just then he reaches up and pulls aside another curtain. Space itself is but a curtain and what's left is pure light, a brilliant light that penetrates you and fills you. It reaches into every cell of your body and your mind. As it fills your mind, you begin to feel one with this light, for this light is all that really is. This light is all you are. Soon there is nothing or no one, just the light.

When you wish, become aware of your body, and of the room in which you are performing this exercise. Stretch a little. Spend some time going over this experience, how it made you feel, and what it did to your awareness, your sense of self and your understanding of what it is to be alive.

11.

We have been considering the transformational aspect of the religious experience, an aspect most often encountered in "mystical" experience. In doing so, much emphasis was placed on "visions" and altered states of consciousness. This has been because they are the most dramatic aspects of religious experience, and the easiest to misunderstand. This emphasis can be misleading, however, in that people with profound experiences of "higher" consciousness still live in the same world that you and I inhabit. In fact, all of the major religious traditions emphasize the importance of "returning to the world." In truth, there is no "return," because if one understands the nature of religious experience, one realizes that it is not an escape *from* reality, but simply a *realization of* our true Nature.

Natural being is our enlightened nature. This being is not something apart from us that we must recapture; we *are* this being. When we make natural being our spiritual home, truth and beauty arise as spontaneous gifts. Perfect knowledge shines into our lives, and our body, mind and sense lead us effortlessly toward enlightenment. The spiritual path is as close as our heartbeat and breath. (Tarthang Tulku, 1981)

5

Dancing

1.

The great cellist, conductor and composer, Pablo Casals, wrote the following memoir as he was beginning his ninth decade,

> For the past eighty years I have started each day in the same manner. It is not a mechanical routine but something essential to my daily life. I go to the piano, and I play two preludes and fugues of Bach. I cannot think of doing otherwise. It is a sort of benediction on the house. But that is not its only meaning for me. It is a rediscovery of the world of which I have the joy of being a part. It fills me with awareness of the wonder of life, with a feeling of the incredible marvel of being a human being. The music is never the

same for me, never. Each day it is something new, fantastic and unbelievable. That is Bach, like nature, a miracle! (Casals, 1970)

2.

Music, singing and dancing play an important role in many people's lives, including in the lives of many senior citizens. In Santa Clara County, California, dancing is so popular and widespread that a special newsletter is published each month informing seniors of the organized dances available to them. There are usually at least 45 organized live music dances available each month, and this does not include the numerous impromptu and recorded music events. A small center, for instance, serving only about 120 seniors a week, has either records playing or someone volunteering time at the piano daily. One larger center has two live band dances each week. Many of the participants are over 70 years of age.

At random some of these seniors were asked why they enjoyed dancing as much as they do. Most answered, "It's fun." Typical of the more thoughtful replies include,

—It makes me feel young again.

—I'm surrounded by old friends. I get to make new ones. I don't have to be lonely anymore.

—When I get out there and move my body, jitterbug and polka, I look around and we don't look so much like old coots anymore. Hell, my daughter's worse off than I am.

—I like especially when we get a good group that can play polkas and ranchero music. I feel alive all the way down to my bones and it gets me all excited, all alive.

These experiences can be understood in terms of cardiovascular response, patterns of socialization and the like, but what is at the heart of the experience of music, and particularly dancing? These people are saying that dancing revitalizes them and atunes them to each other. Pythagoras said that music is the best healer for a sick soul, and common wisdom speaks of music as taming the wild beast. What are the elements of dance and music that give them the power to accomplish these healing tasks?

3.

Melody is a central feature of most music. It is the tune we hum, sing or to which we dance. Melody can be a creation of soul, as in a folk tune, or of spirit, as in a complex symphony, or of the two working together, as in the symphonic compositions of Ralph Vaughan Williams. Oftentimes, and especially in symphonic compositions, music will express the entire range of human emotion and experience, weaving them back and forth, uniting them into a complex whole. For instance, Beethoven's "Missa Solemnis" presents a range of experience from abject melancholy to sublime ecstacy, from beauty and harmony to the ravages of man's inhumanity and war mongering, all united into a complex and profoundly moving whole.

Frequently melody and lyric are intertwined. Sometimes we can remember the tune, sometimes the words, but it usually takes both working together to make the full impact of the song. The words of music can be poetic or quite plain, but they frequently run along rather basic themes. Love, fulfilled or unrequited, longing, praise of beauty, physical, spiritual, personal or of nature, stories of heroes and villains and features of everyday life. In fact, the texts of our songs are frequently text-books of our lives, and our patterns of listening to some songs over and again weave the text-ures, like tapestries, of our inner world.

One of the greatest "musicians" of the Western World was the composer of the epic poems *The Iliad* and *The Odyssey*. While we know that these works were compiled over generations by wandering bards, both individually and in groups, tradition calls the final compiler of the tales Homer. These poems were originally songs, performed to music, probably accompanied by a form of lute or harp. They were dinner entertainment. *The Iliad* is the tale of the heroes of Troy. These heroes live on in memory, come alive at each singing or reading of their stories.

The theme of remembering, an underlying theme in *The Iliad* comes to the forefront in *The Odyssey*. Odysseus, the hero of this epic, is faced with the task of returning home after the sack of Troy. Through his own bragging and curiosity and because of the foolishness of his crew, Odysseus is blown off course and wanders through a mythical realm of perilous adventure. Throughout this adventure he is faced with the task of remembering who he is and his goal of homecoming, as well as with the danger of forgetting. In some ways *The Odyssey* can be seen as Odysseus' "decompression," i.e. his return from being a savage warrior and sacker of cities back to being a peace loving and magnanimous king and husband. In order to accomplish this task, Odysseus has to "remember" his original nature, to "re-member" his life. He was required to take things apart, to encounter each of the major elements of his psyche in symbolic adventures with mythical beings, and to re-integrate them. Remembering as shifting the patterns of life, "re-membering" or re-integrating them and in doing so returning to our original nature.

Many people have written commentaries on Odysseus' path. Some have seen a profound meaning presented clothed in images of this story. These commentators explain that we are all born in a state of unity with Ultimate Reality. This is indeed our Original Nature. In our first days, weeks and months, not to mention the first few years of life, we are faced with the need to survive on this planet, and we lose this original unity. We get hints of it often throughout life, in the special feeling at seeing a magnificent sunset, the special closeness of a loved one, even in a vague sense of longing for "something better." It is our task, like Odysseus', to remember our Original Natures and to return to them, not as babies, but bringing together the full scope of all of our experiences and reintegrating them in an experience of unity with Ultimate Reality.

Music, through lyric and melody, can remind us to remember and give us a tool to aid our "re-membering." As we pay attention to the lyrics which speak to us today, we can gain insight into the movements of our inner lives. As we pay attention to the lyrics which moved us last year, or five, ten, perhaps forty years ago, we can begin to understand the threads of the patterns of our inner life, sung by us and through us. Thus music can offer us an opportunity to reintegrate and restructure our lives to once again reclaim our Natural Selves.

4.

Josh is a great story teller and an even better singer. In fact he sometimes combines the two, changing the old words or creating new words to old tunes much like a wandering minstrel of the Middle Ages. Even though he is in his mid-70's, his voice can still fill medium sized hall. We were talking about music one afternoon when I asked what were his favorite songs. He replied,

> Well its hard to say. There are so many good songs. Even new ones. Not all that rock is bad, even though I don't like much of it, but, hey, I guess our parents didn't like the wild music we were into as kids. My favorites? Let me think... I think there are four songs that I like most. Not because of the songs so much but because each of my wives and I had special songs. Yes, I've been married four times and I loved them all, still do. Just too restless a spirit, I suppose. Me and Mary liked "Come Josephine in my Flying Machine." I guess that shows my age. See, she was sort of afraid of heights, so we'd make kind of a joke of it, you know, "Up, up, a little bit higher. Oh, my!" Martha and I met at a German dance. The first dance we had together was *The Blue Danube*. That's a great waltz. I remember it was played by a trio, a zither, violin and drums. Martha was a great dancer and everytime I waltz I could close my eyes and imagine her with me. We'd dance the night away. She died. After the funeral I played *The Blue Danube* once more and then broke the record. Haven't replaced it yet. Don't plan to. Stella and I liked "The Isle of Capri." She was Italian and we honeymooned there. Very romantic. She was a lot like the tango. Lots of life and love. Now Betsy and I like to sing "What a Difference a Day Made." You know, "My yesterday was blue dear, Today I'm a part of you dear..."

In those few moments, in recollecting a few songs and their lyrics, Josh presented me with a full picture of his life, happiness and grief, passions and fears, a life lived with joy and fullness. The texts of music weaving the textures of his life.

5.

While melody and lyric are important to music, the music they would make by themselves would soon turn boring. Harmony is important, adding color and texture to a composition. Harmony occurs when two or more notes are played simultaneously and the sound produced is a pleasing combination. Musicians have discovered that harmony is frequently intensified if it follows and "resolves" some dissonance. Harmony and dissonance, like that food combination, sweet and sour, depend upon each other to highlight their own natures.

Harmony has another meaning in our culture, one of peace, concord and agreement among people. Utopian communities, places where people are said to live out ideals of brotherhood, have adopted names like New Harmony. In these communities dissonance is not considered a positive value. Through the influence of their ideals and their ethics, these same attitudes have passed into much of our culture as an ideal and a goal. They even permeate business, where the ideal worker is a highly motivated *team player*, and a person with rough edges is definitely *persona non grata*, unless he or she is a genius who will cause the company to make tremendous profits. Furthermore, this viewpoint so permeates our ideals that we apply it to our inner lives. How often we judge our moments of exuberance or of emotion as inappropriate, how often would we like to do away with our false starts, flights of fancy and "silly" whims, and how often do we hold as our ideal one form or another of fitting in with a group! Frequently people speak of the ideal life as one of "wholeness." By this is usually meant a view of life in which all the dissonant aspects have been eliminated or sublimated into a "harmony." This is "wholeness" seen from the viewpoint of "perfectionism" and not from a viewpoint of true "harmony" in which the whole is composed of the mutual interdependence of *all* of its parts.

Lived experience suggests that reality is very different from this questionable ideal. Frequently as we age, the patterns of our lives become more clear. Perhaps repeated occurrences make it more difficult to deny those parts of our personalities we would soon forget, perhaps age brings courage. Nonetheless, we become more aware of aspects of our lives we find dissonant. This can occur in reminiscence groups and, if not treated with polyanna denial can bring much growth and self-acceptance. The same experience is recorded in many of the journals and autobiographies written by thoughtful people in their elderly years, viz. Malcolm Cowley, Florida Scott-Maxwell and Carl Jung. Consider the following quotations from one of the journals of the poet, essayist and playwright, May Sarton,

> For a long time now, every meeting with another human being has been a collision. I feel too much, sense too much, am exhausted by the reverberations after even the smallest conversations...The anguish of my life here—its rages—is hardly mentioned. Now I hope to break through into the rough rocky depths, to the matrix itself. There is violence there and anger never resolved...I wonder whether it is possible at nearly sixty to change oneself radically. Can I learn to control resentment and hostility, the ambivalence, born somewhere far below the conscious level?...There is nothing to be done but go ahead with life moment by moment and hour by hour—put out birdseed, tidy the rooms, try to create order and peace around me even if I cannot achieve it inside me. (Sarton, 1977)

This human experience is a far cry from the sense of "wholeness" taken in a perfectionistic manner. And yet it is very close to the sense of "wholeness" suggested by an understanding of the nature of harmony in music, each more deeply appreciated because of the presence of its opposite. This suggests that everything in life, joy or sorrow, high or low, no matter, all join in the celebration of a dynamic balance which we call life. And it also suggests that these "undesireable" elements of our inner life play a vital role in the overall economy of our personal lives.

6.

Finally, we arrive at rhythm, the beat, that aspect of music one can feel in the bones. Rhythm is an underlying pulse which gives dynamism to a song. In order to dance well, a person must let go of his or her preconceptions and flow with the beat of the music. Perhaps the most pristine form of music is a drum pulsing near a campfire and as such music speaks directly to an instinctual part of every person, directly to the unconscious. Psychologically, the controlling ego must give way to the body and its instinctual rhythms. Ego consciousness and instinctual consciousness begin to dance with each other. Let us examine this phenomenon of beat or pulse more carefully.

Modern physics has discovered that the entire universe is composed of pulsing energy. At the heart of the atom is not something solid but rather vibrating energy. What to us looks like physical matter is "dense" energy vibrating at a slower rate of speed. Consider water. Heat water, i.e. add energy and speed up the level of vibration, and it turns to steam, something which looks immaterial. Cool water, that is, lower the level of vibration, and it turns to ice, a substance of apparently greater materialness than water. Same substance, different appearances, different rates of pulsing or energy. The same is true for all of "matter," including our bodies. (It is interesting to note that this "breakthrough" of modern physics is almost identical to the traditional teachings of Vedantic and Buddhist philosophy.)

Not only is the stuff of which we are made composed of vibrating energy, but also the manner in which it is held together is based on a dynamic pulsing of energy. The body is composed of rhythmic processes following certain definite patterns. There are *circadian* rhythms, rhythms whose cycles take about a day to complete. These include regular patterns of body temperature, hormone levels, urine production, sleep/waking cycles and levels of cognitive and motor performance. There are *infradian* cycles, rhythms whose patterns take longer than a day. These include ovulation and menstruation. In the animal world these patterns include hibernation, in which body temperature and functioning make radical, but regularly predictable, shifts. Finally there are *ultradian* cycles, patterns which occur more frequently than once a day. These patterns include the sleeping pattern, a definite repetition which occurs four to six times during an approximately 8 hour interval of sleep. Not only have these patterns been discovered and documented, but we have also come to understand that the functioning of the brain itself occurs in rhythmic patterns detectable by an EEG as brain wave patterns. In Alpha waves, the brain pulses at 8-12 cycles per second. Beta waves, our normal awake and active state, pulse at 14-30 cycles per second. Theta waves, vibrating at 4-7 cycles per second, are acceptable during sleep and perhaps other altered states of consciousness, but present a problem to someone in an awake state. The human body, not to mention the entire universe, is composed of vibrant, dynamic, pulsing energy, in other words, rhythm.

There is another discovery in the field of physics which is pertinent to this topic. In the mid 1600's, Christian Huygens discovered that two pendulums when mounted side by side would synchronize their movements and swing together in precisely the same rhythm. In fact they would be able to maintain their mutual beat at a level of accuracy far beyond what could mechanically be measured. This has come to be called "entrainment." Furthermore there is a well known biology experiment utilizing two individual heart muscle cells, each pulsing at its own seperate pace. As they are brought closer together, even before they touch, a shift occurs and these individual cells begin to pulse together in the same rhythm. George Leonard took these two basic facts and combines them with the research conducted by Dr. William Condon of the Boston University School of Medicine in which the patterns of human communication were studied in almost microscopic detail. His conclusion brings together the disparate elements of this discussion. He concludes that all human communication is actually a form of entrainment. (Leonard, 1978)

So, in dancing, a body situates itself in space and time. It begins to experience a certain pulsing beat, a rhythm. Perhaps what occurs is a form of entrainment. Two people dancing together to the same ryhthm experience a synchronization of the very rhythms which make up their biological processes. In other words, they share the same pulsing rhythms which constitute consciousness. This is not as radical as it may seem, as born out by the following two examples.

In his biography of the Amazonian shaman Manuel Cordova-Rios, Bruce Lamb describes experiences Cordova-Rios had while training in his art. His teacher would gather a group of men who were suitably prepared, retire to a selected location and mutually consume an hallucinogen called *ayahuasca.* The master shaman would then guide the group by means of chants through a series of *communaly* experienced visions. Without the shaman dictating the contents of the visions, each member of the group experienced the same vision. They actually shared in each other's visions. (Lamb, 1974) That is to say, the manifestations of their consciousness were synchronized. Psychological entrainment.

One day in graduate school one of my professors tried an experiment. The 20 or so of us in the class entered states of deep relaxation. Our professor then played a short piece of music, after which we shared with each other what we had experienced during the music. The exciting part of this experiment was that every person in the room experienced almost identical feelings, and some of us even experienced almost identical images, all without the use of mind altering drugs. We experienced the power of music to create entrainment, a synchronization of not only the body's processes but also the mind's.

Let us return to the drum beats alongside a campfire, or even the rhythm of a polka played in a senior citizens' center. The beat, the pulsing rhythm of the music speaks directly to a deep, primitive, instinctual part of our psyche, directly to the depths of the unconscious. At this level people participating begin to share in the very same state of consciousness and entrainment occurs, that is, their psychological and biological rhythms begin to synchronize. This can take place equally at the drum beating ceremonies of primitive people, at shamanic rituals and at senior centers. At this level we begin to experience the pulse-like nature of all Reality and in a subtle manner we begin to synchronize our own rhythms to the rhythms of our fellow human beings, and perhaps to the rhythms of the dance of life itself.

7.

If the nature of the world is that of a dynamic pulsing reality, then the only constant we can speak of is change itself. This image of the world as change is not a new image, even to Western Culture. Heraclitus, the Greek pre-Socratic philosopher who turned 40 in the 69th Olympiad (504-501 B.C.) is most famous for his dictum, *panta rei kai ouden menei,* everything flows like a river and nothing remains the same. Problems occur when we lose sight of this fundamental aspect of reality and try to freeze things, holding on to some partial aspect of reality for the sake of a feeling of security.

Jaroslav was a 92 year old first generation Estonian immigrant. He had his room filled with jars of herbs, leaves, roots and grasses which he claimed to have brought with him from Estonia. (In a more candid moment he also admitted to gathering many of them near his northern Indiana home.) He had filled his apartment with so much organic matter and had ignored its decomposition and consequent tenancy by a host of living creatures to such an extent that the local health department had the place declared a health hazard and ordered the sheriff's department to clean the place out. Jaroslav fought them off with his cane until he was finally taken to a local psychiatric ward for a 72 hour visit. When he became physically ill, he fought hard to avoid confinement in a convalescent facility, and when he was finally placed there he became profoundly depressed, primarily because the nursing home would not allow him to keep any of his jars of roots.

On the surface, Jaroslav's jars of "Estonian" herbs were a kind of connection to the place which was, in his mind, his real home. Yet their meaning went even deeper. Jaroslav's father was an herbalist, the village healer. Thus these jars contained Jaroslav's connection to his father, and in some way contained his understanding of the healing power of nature and of our need to be rooted in nature. Jaroslav had, however, confused a set of powerful psychological and spiritual truths with their concrete manifestations and he clutched this construct as a kind of "security blanket." He lost touch with genuine healing energies, ever changing and dynamic as they are, and clutched an external form all the way to isolation and profound depression.

Jaroslav is by no means the only person who has tried to block the "ravages of time." I met Estrellita at a neighborhood senior center. Her friends asked me to talk with her because she had not been herself since the death of her husband, almost 6 years ago. Both Estrellita and her husband had been vivacious, outgoing people who enjoyed a steady stream of visitors at their house. Since Fernando's death the socializing ground to a halt and Estrellita was depressed and withdrawn. After a few weeks of working with Estrellita I found an excuse to visit her at her house and discovered part of the reason why she no longer had visitors. Every room of the house was filled with garbage, trash and other collected artifacts, coming to about my shoulder height, somewhat over the head of Estrellita. Pathways were cut through the mess for movement from one room to another. She slept in a chair because her bed was covered with things. I thought of her as a kind of urban woodchuck.

Since the death of her husband, Estrellita could not bring herself to throw anything away. It began with her reticence to part with anything which belonged to him, and then it spread insidiously to other things, finally ending in a compulsion to save everything. Somehow if she could hold onto this "stuff" she wouldn't have to face her husband's death, her terrible feelings of aloneness and her own impending demise. It was an attempt to freeze the flow of things in order to hold on to some point of security. With a few weeks of therapy Estrellita was able to relax her desperate clutching and once again join her friends in the flow of life.

8.

Jaroslav, Estrellita and the countless others like them are not the only ones who try to capture an aspect of reality and hold onto it for their own personal security. They are more visible because of the overt manner in which they go about their "craft," but the underlying dynamic occurs in each of our daily lives. The following exercise may help to bring awareness to this dynamic.

Prepare yourself by sitting in a position conducive to meditation, be that on the floor or in a chair. Make sure your back is straight. Take a few deep breaths and then breathe in a slow and regular manner. Try to focus on your breathing, clearing your mind of all thoughts.

Now begin to think of something which made you angry. It may be a memory of an actual situation or you may imagine a typical situation, but be specific. Notice how the anger arises. Feel where it arises in your body, where perhaps warmth, tightness or discomfort registers. Do not judge or criticize your reactions, simply pay attention to them. Notice how the feeling of anger can occupy almost all of your consciousness. Pay attention to how difficult or easy it is to let go of these images, thoughts or feelings.

Now once again focus upon your breathing, and as you gently bring your mind back to your breath, let your mind grow calm and clear. Now focus upon a sexually arousing situation, actual or imagined. Be specific in your visualization. Pay attention to the feelings which arise. Where do they register in your body? What quality of mind do they engender? Are they like fire? Are they sharp, diffuse, pleasurable, painful, etc.? Notice how these images and feelings can possess almost all of your consciousness. Pay attention to how difficult or easy it is to let go of these images, thoughts and feelings.

Now once again focus upon your breathing, and as you gently bring your mind to your breath, let your mind grow calm and clear. Now visualize a situation from your work life. Perhaps a time of great pressure, of demands for special performance, of a failure or of some other intense situation. Let it be a real or imagined situation, but please be specific about its details. Once again, pay attention to the feelings you experience as they arise within you. Notice their intensities and special qualities. Notice, too, how they fill your consciousness. Pay attention to how easy or difficult it is to let go of these images, thoughts and feelings.

Bring your awareness back to a calm and centered attitude, using your breath to focus your awareness. Now review the last few minutes. Notice how each of the three visualizations generated thoughts and feelings which filled your consciousness. Notice, also, that you created each of those situations. They had no material reality. They were simply created by your mind for this exercise. Notice how your consciousness became filled with these products of your mind and how easy or difficult it was to let them go.

9.

The gods and goddesses of the Hindu Pantheon are envisioned as representatives of aspects of the fundamental nature of Reality.

As such they can offer valuable insights into human nature. One of these figures is Shiva Nataraja, the "Lord of the Cosmic Dance." Shiva Nataraja is depicted as a youthful being, standing on top of a dwarf and a snake, one foot elevated, as in a dance, with four arms, surrounded by a ring of flames. His body roughly assumes the shape of the Sanskrit syllable OM. Joseph Campbell describes some of the significance of the symbolism of Shiva Nataraja,

> The upper right hand of the dancing god holds a little drum shaped like an hourglass, the ryhthm of which is the world-creating beat of time, projecting temporality and thereby the temporal world. The extended left hand holds the flame of spiritual light that burns the veil away, thus annihilating the world and revealing the void of eternity....The god's head, meanwhile, is poised, serene and still, in the midst of all the movement of creation and destruction represented in the rhythm of the rocking arms and slowly stamping right heel. (Campbell, 1974)

OM is usually understood to be the seed syllable, the sound which is the basis of all being. It is the appearance of Shiva, dancing through creation and destruction which brings the world to life.

A dancing god, or perhaps god as dance. But what a dance! All of reality, pulsing and vibrating, is the creation of a Cosmic Mind, and our participation in life is largely due to our own mental projections of reality. We can easily see this when it manifests in insignificant dimensions. For instance, if I awaken in a bad mood, that mood will color my entire day and actually shape my encounters with others. Store clerks will appear to be less helpful and courteous, and they probably will be so. I'm sure I will encounter angry people and more than usually discourteous drivers. Yet if I break that mood, things will shortly be different. In this small sense I "create" the world by mental projections. The message of the Lord of the Dance, however, goes much deeper.

When we begin to pay close attention to our own mental processes we come to realize that the mind is similar to an ocean beach. At one moment the beach is alive with the sight and sound of a large wave pressing towards the shore. A moment later the wave is gone and there is silence. Within seconds another wave breaks for the beach. Minute by minute, day by day this pattern inexorably reasserts itself. So too the mind. A feeling or thought arises and takes possession of all of our attention. Perhaps it is an anxiety, fear or anger. Perhaps a feeling of personal unworthiness. For that one moment it seems as if that thought or feeling is the sum total of reality. We can hold on to some states of mind because they are pleasant to us and we can create inner barricades to keep away from awareness those states we judge as undesirable. We can attempt to fix reality into something solid, but we do so at the price of constant inner vigilance and judgements, judgements which we turn against ourselves. But Reality is not solid and its manifestations pass and are replaced by other thoughts or feelings. Minute by minute, hour by hour, day and night what we perceive as reality is created from some unknown source within our deepest selves and then once again vanishes. If we let go of our judgements and preconceptions we also let go of the self-criticisms which make us miserable, and which keep us from dancing, for Reality is a dance, the Cosmic Dance of Shiva, and we are its invited guests.

6.

Loving

1.

Who can deny the central importance of loving for human life? On the one hand all the great religions have some form of loving or compassion central to their understanding of the nature of man. On the other hand all we have to do is listen to our own hearts to understand how much we need to be loved, and to love. Popular literature is filled with questions of love. Advice columnists instruct us in discerning, as well as doing, it. Pundits discuss selfish vs. selfless love. Men's and women's magazines are constantly debating the role of sex in love. So much has been said about love and loving that one wonders where to even begin another discussion of loving.

Just what is love? Is it a feeling or a state of being? Is it an attempt to fill a need or an unselfish concern for the welfare of the other? Is it freedom or an obsession? And what, if anything, has love got to do with sex? Let us begin by temporarily putting aside all of our beliefs about love. Let us assume that we know nothing of love. Actually, to be more specific, let us put aside the beliefs about love which we have inherited from popular culture, the kind of sentiments you hear when listening to either country-western or popular songs. Let us return to some images of love as found near the beginnings of our culture in Ancient Greece, and some others found in the experiences of people near the ends of their lives.

2.

One of the first images that comes to mind from the classical world is that of the beautiful goddess of love, Aphrodite. This is indeed fitting, for this radiant daughter of the sun is the archetypal power behind most sensual attraction. But other gods and goddesses also love, and their love is expressed very differently. For instance, Artemis, the chaste goddess of virgin nature loves in a much more celibate manner. Let us seek a more fundamental starting point, some image which represents the basic dynamics of love no matter who, or what, is involved. We can find this starting point in the image of the god Eros.

Eros inspired fear in every god and goddess of the Greek pantheon, in other words; he had absolute power over all. Eros is one of the gods most often associated with the powers of creation. In some traditions, Eros was born of fullness and need. Right from his beginning, Eros is seen as joining the opposites. This image of Eros' birth is somehow most appropriate, for in our fullness we glimpse our true human limitedness, and in our neediness we can glimpse the fullness of life.

3.

The Ancient Greeks believed that there were three components to eros, namely *himeros, anteros,* and *pothos. Himeros* is that aspect of eros which is the physical desire for something immediately present. It is that part of eroticism which comes alive when one person is physically attracted to another body. Nor is it necessarily confined to the physical attraction between people. *Himeros* is also present in the emotional life of collectors, be that of butterflies or baseball cards, in their desire to physically possess an object. It can also be present when one is stimulated by a work of art or a rosebush. In other words, whenever we, as spirits and souls incarnated in bodies, are attracted to someone or something, we experience a desire which is in part physical. That is the action of *himeros*. *Anteros* is that aspect of eros generated as a response, our becoming actively engaged with the object of our experience of eros. It is eros as a return of feeling or desire. *Pothos* is very different in its relationship to the object of desire, for *pothos* is...

> the longing towards the unattainable, the ungraspable, the incom-
> prehensible, that idealization which is attendant upon all love and
> which is always beyond capture.... *Pothos* here would refer to the
> spiritual component of love or the erotic component of the spirit...
> the motive force that drives desire onwards, as the portion of love
> that is never satisfied by actual loving and actual possession of the
> object.... This side of eros makes possible living in the world as a
> scene of mythical action, mythologizing life. (Hillman, 1974)

Sometimes pothos is easy to spot. A sixty-four year old nun told me,

> There is an old hymn that haunts me. I can't remember all of the
> words, my memory is not what it used to be, but it calls us exiled
> sons and daughters of Eve. I love life, expecially my life as a sister.
> We have a beautiful home here. I love these flowers. I'm the sister-
> gardener. They give me much pleasure, as does the food and com-
> pany. I was never really much of an ascetic. I still don't enjoy fast-
> ing. But after you've felt God touch you, this life, well... We're in
> exile because our real home, and I know our deepest happiness,
> will only come when we are united with God forever.

Longing for the Divine is indeed one of the most pristine forms of *pothos,* but not by any means its only manifestation. Reggie lost his wife about a year before I met him. He still hadn't gotten over it. He was shattered. He would spend all day brooding, thinking of nothing but her. He knew she was gone forever, even felt it was better for her to be dead than suffer an excruciating death from cancer, but he could find no way to get her out of his mind. Reggie was filled with pothos, longing, for his wife. Reggie's longing for his wife reminded me of Dante's longing for Beatrice. Dante, however, had learned to relate to the object of his unattainable longing through images and the imagination, and thus created a great work of art. Reggie was still stuck with a concrete, i.e. material, object of desire, and thus his experience ate him away.

Longing for the Divine, longing for an unattainable other, these are both forms of an aspect of Eros. *Pothos* makes us feel our inner life with an exquisite sharpness, not unlike Eros-Cupid's infamous arrows. If we attune ourselves to that inner reality, we can allow it to express itself through us into various forms, such as poetry, music, prose, ceramics, etc. *Pothos* is, or can be, a powerful mover and creator of inner life, a fitting incarnation for Eros, one of the primal forces of creation.

4.

We can find another manifestation of pothos in a seemingly unlikely place, namely on the streets of our inner cities. "Street People" are those who willingly eschew home, apartment or permanent shelter for a life lived primarily on the streets. These are not the evicted victims of circumstance, but those who willingly live in parks, under viaducts, in abandoned or dilapidated pick-ups and condemned passageways. They are frequently on the move, usually with only a post office box number, and are very suspicious of outsiders. There is very little scholarly literature about these people, a testament to their skills at avoiding outsiders' probing questions. Let us meet one of these people.

Willie was somewhere in his upper sixties. He was not an alcoholic, nor was he psychotic, but he was poor, living on a meager social security check. He chose not to apply for additional benefits because that would require establishing a permanent residence, and Willie didn't want to be pinned down. Month after month, year after year, every time I met Willie he would repeat, almost more to himself than to me,

> Boy, things are sure going to be different when I get my next check. Yep, I'm going to move to _____. I got friends over there. Got my eye on an apartment and a girlfriend to share it with. No more sleeping on cardboard and carrying around my stuff in a plastic bag. You just wait and see...

Willie died before he ever actualized his dream, but that dream, that spirit of *pothos*, kept Willie alive for quite a few years.

James Dickey seems to have captured this longing in a poem entitled, "Bums, On Waking." In this poem Dickey writes of the inner lives of the street bums. He comments on their absolute commitment to life itself, a commitment thrown into the face of insecurity and doubt. Who will wake them, friend or foe? Or will they even awake? It matters not. Though they walk the narrow line of destruction, though their mattress might be a park bench or their pillows stone curbs, they live for the hope of the first light of dawn. (Dickey, 1978) A spirit of longing keeps these people alive and on the move, pursuing some vision which will never, can never, materialize; but which enlivens them, a vision which, as Dickey portrays, is essentially spiritual longing.

5.

Himeros, anteros, pothos—powerful movements of the human psyche, powerful traces of Eros. Now let us shift this discussion to another aspect of love, namely sexuality. Our society, no doubt in a well-founded reaction to Victorian rigidity, has brought sex into the open. It's ok to be sexy. We now have permission to experience orgasm without guilt, and we no longer have to pay certain psychological prices for sex. Sex has been freed! In other words, sex has lost its taboo quality. No doubt this has helped overcome much neurosis and has freed many people from unnecessary torment, but it is also important to understand what has been lost in this process, namely taboo.

Taboo is not merely a set of arbitrary social injunctions. Taboos are intended as protection. They are indicators that one is approaching something of immense power, something which may be beneficial to those who approach properly, and highly destructive to the unprepared, namely, something sacred. Many societies have understood the relationship between sex and the sacred—a relationship we have lost. In India, in the redeeming god Shiva's worship are prominently found physical representations of the penis and vulva, the lingam and yoni. For centuries Tantric yoga has used the mysteries of male-female sexuality to lead a person to enlightenment. In our own culture, the Greeks used an erect phallos as a representation of Hermes. These erect penises can still be seen on tombstones throughout Greece as well as on pediments lining the streets of the ancient holy city of Delos. Furthermore, the great initiation rites, those ceremonies which taught people the deepest truths about the nature of the universe, have been associated with sexuality.

Sex, therefore, is a doorway to the sacred. Sexual experience, if entered into deeply enough, can be an experience of the Divine. Eros is a deity of creation not simply because he creates desire, even if that desire is for the ineffable, nor is he a deity merely because he can create new life through his sexual joinings. Eros is a God because he leads us to an experience of his Divinity in bodies and souls, that is if we allow ourselves to experience the imagination and the body of Eros.

6.

Word is out—older people are loving people. They even enjoy sex. From bumper stickers boasting "sexy senior citizen" to afternoon talk shows, elder sex is beginning to go public. Sex is an important part of loving and you don't have to check in your sexuality when you hang up your lunch box for the last time. But some images of later life sexuality have been around for a long time, even to the point of existing primarily as stereotype. It can be amazing to meet someone in the flesh who almost perfectly embodies a sterotype.

Gregor, in his late 70's, was the "archetypal dirty old man." Frequently, while still married, Gregor would tell his wife he was going to play cards with the boys, leaving home at about 10:00 A.M. and returning after 4:00 P.M. He really spent the time in "adult" theaters. Sometimes he went to the live stage shows and hung around the dancers' dressing rooms, hoping to win a date or at least smell the dancers' body odors as they returned from their performances. He had a penchant for prostitutes, the younger the better, and was on more than one occasion the victim of some over-zealous tip taking. Gregor decided it was time for some counseling because he was having trouble maintaining an erection with a particularly attractive young lady. It seems the sweet thing laughed at his shrivelled organ. The humiliation hit home.

Therapy must have been a success for Gregor because everytime he saw me after our first session, he gave me a "thumbs up" sign. One day I asked him what he meant by that, and he replied, "Why, there ain't nothin' in this ol' worl' sweeter than the smell of yer thumb after you pull it out of a broad's _____."

The next time I saw Gregor was for some court ordered therapy. The old man had stationed himself at the bottom of a spiral staircase so that he could look up the dresses and skirts of the women who used the stairs. The judge sentenced Gregor to mandatory therapy when he pleaded innocent, stating that no harm was done in seeing a few tushies wiggle. Besides, Gregor added in his own version of impeccable logic, they all wore underpants.

Gregor's personal life was a shambles. His clothes were usually dirty, his body frequently a host for lice due to his refusal to bathe, his health was poor and his teeth had rotted away. The prostitutes who would finally be cajoled or bribed into his service usually charged extra because of his personal hygiene. Eventually Gregor's wife had left him for a younger man, a fellow in his late 60's who was devoted to her. Alone, impotent and without any significant personal relationship, Gregor the lecher.

There are, in fact, actual lechers, "dirty old men and women." Stereotypes, rumors and humor are based upon these characters, both real and imagined. But why do these stereotypes still exist? And why are they so powerful, forming a kind of modern mythology? The lecher is all *himeros*, sexuality turned towards a material object. Perhaps lechery is graphic symbol of the manner in which the modern person lives his or her life. Every person can be counted, every action can be categorized. These are fundamental assumptions of our society. But in order to maintain these assumptions, people and acts must be reduced to a quantifiable, i.e. material, mode of existence. In this respect there is little difference between sterile death wards and pornographic magazines. Perhaps. And yet it is also possible that the emotional power associated with the images of lechery points to some reality still hidden in the depths of our psyches, something so powerful that we are still ill at ease in speaking about it directly, a reality that manifests itself in images and mythology.

7.

Among the last works of art created by Pablo Picasso was a series of 347 etchings entitled "347 Gravures." One of these plates, numbered Etching I.31.8.68, is a representation of a theme which is frequently found in Picasso's oeuvre. On the left side of this print an artist and his model are in ecstatic copulation. On the right side is a dried-out celibate bishop, robed in ecclesiastical garments, leering lecherously as voyeur. The unrelatedness in the celibate's sexuality is striking.

Far from being an attack on organized religion, this etching and other similar works by Picasso are powerful and deep statements about sexuality and creativity. Dried-up, impotent, un-related, the bishop now experiences sexuality by means of voyeurism and lechery. Here sexuality is seen without the dimension of relationship which Eros brings. It is experienced primarily as a work of imagination, of fantasy. This etching, like the two heads of the Roman god Janus, presents the two essential aspects of sexuality—relatedness and imagination.

Most of us recognize the presence of Eros by its powerful physical urges, but what of its fantasy life? If the physical acting out of sexuality is blocked, a powerful sexual activity takes place. Imagination comes to the forefront, frequently in a torrent of nearly obsessive images. It is true that we as bodies have definite needs for sensual and sexual experience and expression. Nonetheless, sexuality in its most powerful form is primarily a matter of psychological fantasy. To forget or suppress this imaginative activity is to rob ourselves of a creative activity essential to our well being. This message is Gregor's gift to us.

The creative artist, constantly seeking to manifest beauty in a new form, is continually inspired by an erotic connection. Eros is the source of creativity. However, this eros must be allowed to penetrate the psyche, to fertilize the imagination in order to bring forth new forms. If only the physical, material aspects of the erotic connection are allowed to exist, then the regenerative, creative and even spiritual aspects of life wither. Creativity becomes literalized into production, art becomes objects to be collected or displayed in museums, relationships become quantifiable acts which can be performed, manipulated and improved, and sexuality becomes shriveled up, hardly more than some form of lechery.

Gregor's sexuality neither plummeted to the depths of his soul nor soared to the heights of his spirit. It was caught in a soulless bog of acted out materialism. Seeking to right itself, Gregor's inner life burst forth in a torrent of imagination. Though his consciousness was totally sexualized and his imaginative powers fully activated, Gregor lacked a vital dimension, the door to creative fullness. His impotent lechery could have become the opening to a rich life of the imagination and a greater sense of relatedness. Where Michaelangelo saw the divine beauty of the human form, Gregor saw tushies wiggling. Where Picasso saw the fertility of the creative process, Gregor saw pornographic images on a six foot screen. Where a sexualized imagination could energize and regenerate a person, Gregor had the bittersweet taste of young prostitutes. And Gregor's sexuality became a symptom of a great suffering precisely because he sought to move it from the realm of imaginal fantasy into that of physical acting out. But sexuality is first and foremost an act of the imagination and it must abide in that fertile realm of the psyche or it will wither and die. Unlike the creative artist who seeks reflection and depth, pursuing images and spirit, the dirty old man is trapped in a literalized, materialized world, devoid of contact with psyche or spirit. But in this respect, the dirty old man differs little from the average man or woman of our culture. It is only that the manifestations of his pain are more extreme.

8.

It's really hard to describe. Sure I left my body, but I was sensing things with my body. Then it happened, like a bright light. You know once I touched a live wire, you know, trying to save some money and do the wiring myself, and it was the same kind of light. It's just like having sex, and orgasm, when it's really good.

Maurice was about 62 years old. He was a rather unsophisticated, not well-read construction worker who was just "brought back" from a cardiac arrest. In describing his near death experience Maurice used an interesting comparison, one which I had heard a few times before in working with dying elderly. I prompted him to expand his descriptions.

What's an orgasm like? Hell, don't you know? Ok, Ok, I'll try to describe it step by step like you ask. Well, its usually in the middle of things, if you know what I mean. The tension starts to build. I can feel myself hard and it gets sort of itchy or burning like. Then my whole skin gets sensitive. It's like Ellie could set me off no matter where she touched me. Then all of a sudden its like I see my thing, not that I'm looking at it, just sort of in my head, and its huge, like bigger than I could even imagine and its ready to explode. I feel it first down there, then sort of all over and I sort of go blank. I'm looking into this burst of light, like I said, sort of when I touched that live wire and had 220 volts going through me. I don't know, I mean I can't describe it. It's like I'm not in my body yet I'm in my body, but it sure feels good.

I remember a college professor telling us that the French call an orgasm "la petite mort," the little death. It is abundantly clear from Maurice's description of an orgasm how essential is the imagination. It is encoded in this very body. Jung spoke of an image as the psychic component of an instinct, and an instinct as the body component of an image. When Maurice's sexuality was most aroused, it moved into image, and image, in turn, moved his body towards its completion. Let us pursue this material in greater depth.

Maurice likened an orgasm to his experience of being shot through with 220 volts of electricity. Both times he had experienced a vision of a tremendous white light, and both times he had described himself as both physical and as something else. And both of these experiences were similar to an experience of his own death, when he was "released" from his body, yet he somehow still felt a part of it.

At one moment, Maurice's consciousness became pure light, that is pure energy. His experience of himself was that of pure energy. That is also the way in which he experienced his body, not as an inert mass of materials, but as a dynamic field of energy. This would not surprise someone professionally engaged in quantum physics. These scientists, people who probe into the nature of the atoms which constitute our world, have long been saying that what looks like matter is but energy vibrating at a slower speed. This is not really so hard to understand. Consider an ice cube. It looks more like "matter" than water, and much more "material" than steam, yet we know that all three of these are really the same chemical compound. Well, it is a little more challenging to try to envision a human body not as material but as vibrating energy. And yet, for centuries Tibetan Buddhists and Tantric Yogis have been saying that things only look "real." But here was a 62 year old French-American construction worker experiencing these profound realities!

Sex can teach us much about our basic reality. It is a time during which we are operating near the peak of our powers, and a time during which our ego is close to letting down its defenses. And here is where imagination enters. Imagination is central to sex because it begins the process of dis-identifying ourselves from "physical, material" aspects of reality. Sex works because imagination begins to move our consciousness away from the physical body. And yet the paradox is that this same activity brings alive our physical bodies, or so it seems. Rather, what happens is that we experience ourselves as pure energy, and it is this contact with our true identity which spills over and revitalizes all other dimensions of our being.

Thus sex, if experienced fully and consciously, can lead a person to a realization of the most profound truths of the universe. This is the sacred function of sex.

9.

"La petite mort." How fitting a description for love. Maybe we can understand this more fully if we contrast love with one of its opposites, anger. Consider this dialogue between a therapist and a 68 year old man suffering from depression and impotence.

"I don't like myself when I'm angry. Sometimes I even get mad at myself for getting mad in the first place."

"What's it like when you get angry?"

"Well first I kind of feel tense, here, like a churning in my stomach. Then, I'm not exactly sure how it happens, but I'm yelling or shouting, or maybe sometimes throwing things. I can put on quite a scene."

"I'll bet you get people's attention."

Carl laughed a bit, "You'd better believe it! Sometimes I even surprise myself."

"You seem very energized as you're telling me this, face red, hands moving around. Carl, it makes me wonder if you don't really enjoy being angry."

After a pause Carl chuckled and said, "It does make me feel alive again. I really get to feeling my oats when I'm angry."

Anger can make us feel strong, alive. It is my anger and, in anger, it is I who make a powerful impact on the world. But what about love? Love makes us feel tender and vulnerable. Love feels as if it comes to us, or through us. We feel it as a gift, and we fear that gifts can be taken back. We know that love cannot be willed, and that makes our egos feel powerless. In fact, rather than actually causing love, our ego usually does things that get in its way.

Love is indeed "la petite mort" because it represents a kind of death, a letting go of our strivings and schemings, a relinquishing of ego. Christianity speaks of love as "It is no longer I (my ego) who lives, but Christ (i.e. love) who lives in me." Buddhists say that compassion (love) is the natural state of Buddha (non-ego Mind). The Greeks said that Eros (love) would drive a person mad (out of their normal ego identity.) Whatever the words, the reality is there, powerfully. It is a reality we desire in the deepest recesses of our beings. It is also a reality we fear with all the clutching energy of our ego.

10.

The following exercise is a very traditional practice for increasing love in your life. It will also help you experience what happens to the ego when your being is filled with love. Pay very careful attention to the following exercise and especially to whatever goes on in your body, mind and awareness. Notice especially what is easy and what is difficult to do.

Find a quiet place, sit comfortably, preferably with your back straight and somewhat relaxed. Breathe deeply and slowly exhale. Notice where you are holding tension and let it go. Imagine that you are breathing in a warm relaxing breath of air. Send it to wherever you notice tension in your body. Let its warmth and gentleness massage that tension out of your body. Let it pass out of your body with your next breath out.

Think of someone you love. Picture that person if you can. With all your heart and mind repeat the following phrases for about 30 seconds. "I wish you joy. I wish you peace. I wish you happiness. I wish you love."

Now picture yourself. Let yourself be surrounded by a loving presence or a white light. Repeat the following for about 30 seconds. "I wish you joy. I wish you peace. I wish you happiness. I wish you love."

Now picture the people with whom you live, or your neighbor. Repeat the following for about 30 seconds. "I wish you joy. I wish you peace. I wish you happiness. I wish you love."

Now picture all of the people in your city. Repeat the following for about 30 seconds. "I wish you joy. I wish you peace. I wish you happiness. I wish you love."

Now picture all of the people in your state. Repeat the following for about 30 seconds. "I wish you joy. I wish you peace. I wish you happiness. I wish you love."

Now imagine all of the people in the country in which you live. Repeat the following for about 30 seconds. "I wish you joy. I wish you peace. I wish you happiness. I wish you love."

Now imagine all of the people in your hemisphere, all of the people who live either north or south of the equator. Repeat the following for about 30 seconds. "I wish you joy. I wish you peace. I wish you happiness. I wish you love."

Now imagine all of the people in the world. Repeat the following for about 30 seconds. "I wish you joy. I wish you peace. I wish you happiness. I wish you love."

Now picture all the life forms, birds, animals, plants, microscopic forms, anything and everything that lives. Repeat the following for about 30 seconds. "I wish you joy. I wish you peace. I wish you happiness. I wish you love."

Repeat this exercise as often as you wish. Notice the changes which occur in your awareness as you do this exercise with increasing frequency.

11.

Robert and Julie met while working on a charity's fund raising committee. Robert liked Julie's hair. It was soft, fluffy, and its ends sort of played around her neck. He liked Julie's face, too, perceiving her full lips as sensuous. He wondered if Julie, a former nun, was still a virgin. Julie liked the way Robert cut through so much philosophizing and took charge of the details of raising money. She thought him insightful and caring. She hardly noticed that he was always impeccabley dressed.

Soon they began to date. Neither could remember who asked first. It was simply the next step after post-meeting coffee breaks. Soon Robert began to fantasize about the size of Julie's breasts. He began to notice the fragrances women were wearing, and how he preferred Julie's to most other perfumes. Julie had her fantasies, too, only they were more about being held in Robert's arms and of having stimulating discussions.

Robert and Julie got married. Their honeymoon seemed to last over a year. Robert revelled in Julie's body with a delight which even he found unusual. Julie began to enjoy buying sensuous lingerie, as much for its feeling on her skin as for Robert's delight. Robert, on his part, enjoyed the lengthy discussions the two of them engaged in so often.

Things began to change somewhere in the second year of their marriage. Julie began to notice that Robert could be quite pig-headed, in fact, at times irrational, stubborn and bigotted. She began to feel that maybe Robert was not all she had thought him to be, but she was growing to enjoy the different moods and ways of sex. Sometimes she feared that all she wanted from Robert was sex, but her body would not let this thought distract her for long.

Robert began to tire of sex. Actually he still enjoyed sex, but he was also wanting something else, something more. True enough he experienced good orgasms, in fact very powerful orgasms, but he also began to want something more lasting, some sort of union, or communion. Even though he was perfectly happy with his intelligent and very attractive wife, he began to experience a restlessness. There were days during which he much preferred talking with his wife to having sex with her.

Robert and Julie began to have fights. She bristled at his pig-headedness, he at her always wanting him around. Occasional tiffs became regular occurrences. They began couples therapy, during which they learned much about themselves. They also learned how they expected each other to somehow fill a hole within their own psyche. And they learned skillful ways to help each other. Robert learned how Julie needed to be in touch with the physical world and with her own body, and he helped her understand and feel good about that. Julie realized how Robert wanted, yet found it very difficult, to deal with emotional and spiritual realities. She provided him with support and encouragement.

12.

Eros is a tricky sort of fellow. His arrows seems to get a person from behind, i.e. in a blind spot. Eros will use *himeros* to capture the attention of those who are caught on a physical, material level of life, but soon that *himeros* will turn into *pothos,* a thirst for the immaterial Wholly Other. And those who devalue the material aspects of life—perhaps they will be caught by "spiritual" attractions, but soon they will be lead to the realities of an embodied life on this planet. And sometimes Eros is even more direct—the professor who falls in love with a whore, and vice-versa.

In truth, the mysteries of Love bring us time and again to one of the most fundamental of the mysteries of human life—that we are a strange mixture of material and immaterial, body and soul, finite and infinite. To stand in either half of this polarity is to miss the excitement, beauty and challenge of being human. But Eros strives to balance things out, even if it takes a few tricks to accomplish his goal, for it is the task of Love to keep us aware of and relating to the totality of life.

7.

On Archetypes and Stereotypes

1.

We have met many people in the previous chapters of this book and, hopefully, have come to understand how each person is a unique human being. We have even seen how people could be exhibiting similar behaviours while still experiencing life and its meaning in a way different from any other human being. We know these facts to be true, and yet there are times when individually and collectively we act differently. We group people into classes and impute traits to them. In other words, at one time or another, just about every person has stereotyped some one or some group of people.

2.

Try to visualize the following scenario and quickly note your first reaction:

You are sitting in an urban park on a warm spring afternoon. You notice an old man coming toward you. His hands are in the pockets of his black raincoat. He has a couple of days growth of beard. He sits on the other side of the bench on which you're sitting.... Now, who is this man?

I have begun numerous workshops across the country with this question. Here are some of the most common responses:

—A dirty old man.

—I wonder if he's going to offer me a candy bar.

—Wally Walnetto. (A classical "dirty old man figure" from Rowan and Martin's television show "Laugh In.")

—Must be some widower who just lost his wife and is in grief.

—Some retired fellow with lots of time on his hands and no way to fill it.

The scenario has been recounted from a real life experience. I met this enigmatic character in San Francisco's Golden Gate Park a few years ago. Here's how it ended: ...The man reached into his pocket and retrieved a copy of Plato's *Symposium*. We sat there for some time, he was reading and I was watching ducks swim by, before we began to talk. The man was a recently retired high school wood shop teacher, still married, now enjoying his leisure by catching up on all the reading he hadn't had time for in his active years of teaching.

3.

Stereotypes abound, based partially on past experience, partially on collective prejudice and partially on projections of the unacceptable elements of one's own inner life. In other words, if I am uncomfortable about some aspect of my self and I keep it buried deep in my soul, chances are it will sneak out as a "projection" onto someone else. For instance, I once counseled a Southern Baptist Minister who saw the devil's licentiousness in almost every young woman. As we worked together this God fearing man struggled with a terrible demon in his own soul. It turned out that he had an eye for pretty women, a trait his parents tried to whip out of him and of which he was very embarrassed. Because he couldn't deal with his own nature and the conflicts it caused him, he repressed it, tried to shove it down so far that it would go away, but it didn't. In fact, it came back in quite an underhanded manner, in his private and public judgements on just about every attractive young woman. Obviously this poor man isn't the only person guilty of projections. Consider white America's racial stereotyping of its black population, its hispanic population and now of its Indo-Chinese immigrants. Consider average America's view of the chronically mentally ill. The list can go on and on. Projections seem to be a part of everyday life, and stereotypes are a form of projection.

The elderly are an easy target for stereotypes. Consider your own views of the elderly. Are they chronically ill, bodies falling apart on a one-way slide downhill? Are they poor and destitute living in hidden hovels? Or perhaps wealthy sun worshippers on the Florida Gold Coast? Dried up and sexless or dirty old lechers? Do they spout old fashioned drivel, or are they Wise Old Men and Women? To some degree these are all stereotypes. That is not to say that an individual over 65 won't fit into one of these categories. They are stereotypes because these pictures of older adults are so commonly held that they shape the way we think about older people and the manner in which we tend to perceive them, individually and as a group. Perhaps they arise from our collective and individual discomforts with the aging process. But they also have roots in a reality much more profound than these individual aspects. In order to understand this reality we will need to take a short digression.

4.

Carl Gustav Jung was born on July 26, 1875. By the time he died, 86 years later on June 6, 1961, he had gained a reputation as one of the world's foremost, and perhaps most controversial psychologists. Jung developed his understanding of human nature from daily contact with hundreds of patients, and from intense scrutiny of his own inner workings. In his professional practice Jung had analysed over 67,000 dreams, his own and his patients'. He noticed patterns in this material as well as similar patterns in other products of the human psyche, e.g., art, mythology, literature, religion, etc. His theories stem from this empirical contact with the living psyche.

For Jung, as for Freud, the psyche is part conscious and part unconscious. In fact, the unconscious is probably more extensive than is our own limited conscious awareness. How does a person become aware of the unconscious? For Jung, again as for Freud, dreams and fantasies provide the starting point. At these times our ego drops its role as coordinator and protector of consciousness, and some of "the other side" can sneak into our awareness. What surfaces are primarily *images*. Jung wrote:

> ...it should be clear that the psyche consists essentially of images.
> It is a series of images in the truest sense, not an accidental juxtaposition or sequence, but a structure that is throughout full of meaning and purpose; it is a picturing of vital activities. (Jung, C.W. 8:618)

For Jung the inner life is a structure with meaning, essentially a structure composed of images. These images form groups, circling around some central image. Some of these clusters or complexes relate almost entirely to an individual's personal life. Others are more universal in nature. For instance, every culture, every society and every individual has some image of "mother." Specific forms and images of "mothering" will differ from culture to culture and from individual to individual, but "mother" is a universal. Jung called these collective images archetypes or archetypal images. He wrote:

Archetypes are, by definition, factors and motifs that arrange the psychic elements into certain images, characterized as archetypal, but in such a way that they can be recognized only for the effects they produce. They exist preconsciously, and presumably they form the structural dominants of the psyche in general. (Jung, C.W. 11:222)

...the archetypes are as it were the hidden foundation of the conscious mind.... Archetypes are systems of readiness for action, and at the same time images and emotions. (Jung, C.W. 10:53)

Archetypes "reside" in a very deep level of the psyche. This discovery is one of Jung's major contributions to Western psychology. At this level of the unconscious, each individual shares much in common with all of humanity. The numerous and powerful images which arise from this level frequently have an impersonal quality about them. For example, dream images from this realm frequently appear as mythological beings or as abstract mandalas. The content of these dreams, while channeled through an individual psyche, is of a collective nature. These images may have just as easily appeared in any person's dreams or fantasies. Jung called this level of the psyche the "collective unconscious."

In the past the archetypes of the collective unconscious were brought to consciousness in images of the gods and goddesses of the great mythologies. For the West, Zeus, Hera, Apollo, Hermes, Dionysus, Aphrodite, Hephaistos, Athena, along with all the other characters of mythology made this deep and profound layer of the psyche available to consciousness. For instance, a place was allowed to the instinctual, sexual part of life through the images and activity of Aphrodite. Today the ancient gods and goddesses have died, that is their images seem to contain little if any power. But these psychic realities remain alive, surfacing in the archetypal images of our dreams, fantasies and behaviours. Jung is often quoted as having said that the gods and goddesses of ancient days are now found in the sufferings of modern man's soul.

There is another way in which these archetypal patterns show themselves, another way in which they unconsciously influence our lives, and that is through stereotypes. As we saw earlier stereotypes occur because of a process called projection. Sometimes these projections are not simply personal in nature, but rather collective. We are now ready to see this mechanism in action, focusing upon the god or archetype "Kronos" and its role in producing many of our unconscious stereotypes of older people and of aging.

5.

One of the common stereotypes of aging is that old age is a time of being shriveled, withered and wrinkled. W.B. Yeats has written a short but poignant poem entitled, "The Old Men Admiring Themselves in the Water," in which he compared old men to twisted thorn trees beside a river, their hands looking more like claws. Those old men look into the water and they see their reflection. Dismayed by the reflections of their bodies ravaged by time, they reflect upon the inexorable movement of the water, lamenting that everything beautiful is like this river—it changes, drifting away (Yeats in Sanders, et al., 1967).

Another cultural stereotype is that old age is a time of drying up and decaying. The ancients attributed senescence to a drying of the humors. (Onians, 1973). Even the inner life can wither, and relationships can dry on the vine. Old age can also be seen as a drying up of sexuality. The old man shriveled up and impotent, the old woman dry and uninterested in sex— these are perhaps the most common of the stereotypes of aging. Almost equally common, at least in terms of humor, is the image of the old man as lechery, the Dirty Old Man.

Another cultural image, one of a more positive nature, is that of the Wise Old Man or Woman. T.S. Eliot, one of the most important of the modern poets used this image in poetry of great intensity and depth. In "The Wasteland," Eliot used the image of the dried-up and impotent old king as an image of our entire patriarchal culture. Only in a stereotypical world does quantity of experience necessitate wisdom and understanding and length of life guarantee meaningful productivity. Something more is needed, some sort of nurturing of a depth dimension. Eliot furthered these wise, knowing the patterns of how things are meant to be. But Eliot pointed out that such knowledge is at best limited and transitory and at worst but a silly caricature. Paradigms change, self-understanding develops, and old knowledge, not to mention old people, can simply look silly. Is this the reward we attain for the struggles of a long life? Eliot offered hope for better. If we abandon our beliefs of how things are, abandon the comfort of our stereotypes, we can live each day, each moment, with profound intensity. Forsaking our illusions of security, we can move into the Unknown and discover the real possibility of love and a deep communion with Reality itself.

In our stereotyped way of seeing the elderly, we see isolation, depression and despair. We see the inexorable loss of friends and faculties, a gradual, irreversible decline. But in truth depression can strike at any age, nor are most old people depressed. And while death seems to be more a factor in our lives as we age, perhaps this is only because we do such a good job of blocking it out of our awareness while we are younger. Then there is the image of grandma or grandpa, spaced out on the porch "contemplating." Perhaps. But there are at least as many grandpas and grandmas leading healthy, active and loving lives. We don't usually think of these people because of the unconscious power of our stereotypes, of the archetypal images playing through our imaginations. But what archetype is behind all of this? Is there an archetype of the stereotypes of aging?

6.

Most of us are familiar with the major characters in Greek and Roman mythology. We know of Hera's jealousy and Zeus's escapades, or Artemis's chastity and Apollo's clear light of reason, etc. These gods and goddesses have clearly defined personalities and sensitivities. Let us spend time with a different god, one who is perhaps not as well known but whose images are of great importance in understanding how we unconsciously categorize and stereotype old people. Let us examine the image complex of the god Kronos, called by some the Senex, i.e. the Old Man.

Kronos is a Titan. In other words, he comes from a time before the well-defined Olympian deities, Zeus, Hera, etc. were on the scene. The

Titans were brutish, overpowering and overreaching. In our society's popular imagination, i.e. stereotyping, motorcycle gangs are Titans of sorts, uncouth, ruffians who obey their own laws based on the dominance of strength. Old age could be a time of defeat by an ill-defined but powerful enemy, or it can be seen as simply a natural continuation of life. When we feel that old age is an inevitable and overpowering backdrop to all of life, a time of decay, despair, meaninglessness and isolation, we are looking at aging through a Titanic perspective. In other words, this archetypal pattern is quietly at work deep in our unconscious life, shaping our ideas and attitudes about aging into its own archetypal patterns. We experience this process as stereotyping old age and the elderly.

Kronos' parents are Ouranos and Gaia, Sky and Earth. Kronos is a figure suspended between sky and earth, spirituality and materialism, imagination and literalism. Kronos is tormented by this inner division in his character and frequently falls prey to depression. In the previous chapters we have seen many examples of the split between imagination and literal enactment in the lives of the elderly. In fact this aspect of the Kronos Complex pervades and permeates our entire society, at least since the days of Descartes. We can also see this tension shape our views of the elderly in more subtle ways. For example, old people are supposed to be more "religious." They are supposed to be facing death and consequently are primarily concerned with less material aspects of life. After all, you can't take it with you. People are still frequently surprised to see a very active 70 year old still interested in life, business, etc. These active elderly frequently receive extended press coverage as if active life after retirement is something out of the ordinary. They have even been called "stereotype breakers." We shall return to the question of depression later.

Throughout most of the images of Kronos we see the mark of his birth in an unparalleled contradictory nature, for instance he is represented equally by the lecherous goat and the celibate, and he can represent both the principles of abstract justice and extreme sadism. It does not take much reflection for us to remember that until recently, and perhaps still now, most people viewed old age as a time when sex was over. Old people were said to be dried up, sexless, chaste, that is, unless the person was a dirty old man or lecherous woman. Our images or memories of grandpa or grandma are of the sexlessness of chocolate chip cookies and lemonade, as opposed to "sexy senior citizens." This splitting off of sexuality from our collective images of aging is the stereotyping work of the senex archetype.

Kronos' father, Ouranos, frightened by a prophet's prediction that one of his own children would usurp his throne and seize power, buried all his children at birth in the bowels of the earth. Kronos' mother played a trick on his father and saved one child. When Kronos finally assumed power, he followed the example of his old man, this time swallowing his children alive. The senex functions by repressing material it fears, relegating it to the bowels of the unconscious or by swallowing it, making it so much a part of the conventional order of things that it loses its spark of change and consequent threat. (Stein, M., 1973) Overt manifestations of this power struggle between generations or between "old orders" and "new orders," manifest in the power struggles of institutions, corporations, government and families, in fact in any situation in which a "new way" threatens the "old order" of things. However, this trait also shapes our stereotype of the elderly. One day spent in a senior citizens center will give ample evidence that some elderly people are more open to new experiences and more liberal regarding political and social issues than many young people, but our society communally holds a stereotypical view of old people as stodgy conservatives who desperately, or powerfully, cling to the old ways and traditions.

Kronos, in league with his mother, overthrew his father by castrating him. Kronos dropped his father's gentials into the sea from which sprang the goddess Aphrodite. Aphrodite is the great goddess of love, blinding man and woman alike, accomplishing her deeds through the powerful imaginations and fantasies of sexuality. When the senex has difficulty with something, he attempts to cut it off by repression. Once pushed into the unconscious, the repressed material begins to grow in the imagination and fantasy life. Energy builds. In time, a full scale depression can overtake a person. The work of the senex. "I don't know why Aunt Edna won't talk to Uncle Harry. I know it makes them both miserable to feud with each other, and its over something so silly that happened years ago." Who hasn't thought of old people as depressed, brooding upon old hurts, real or imagined, until they build to seething resentments. It is a simple fact that people of all ages fall prey to such behavior, but it is also true that in our imaginations we associate this behavior with old people more frequently than with adults "in the prime of life."

After years of supreme power, Kronos' son Zeus led a rebellion and usurped his father's power. Zeus did not, however, kill his father, but he banished Kronos to the farthest reaches of the universe, the "Isle of the Blest," where he would reign over his own kingdom for all eternity, a reign called "The Golden Age." Artistic representations of this scene frequently show Kronos as depressed and brooding, ruminating about his past days of glory. Perhaps one of our society's most hallowed image of the elderly is grandpa and grandma, sitting in their rocking chairs on the front porch, reminiscing about "the good old days." Seeing pictures of senior citizens picketing their local legislature, forming political action groups or circulating petitions, or starting new businesses still jars us a bit. The stereotypes run deep. But this archetypal based stereotype even plays through the elderly themselves when, for instance, they name a citizens' group "The Golden Agers."

When the Romans adopted Greek mythology, they fused the images of Kronos to those of their own god Saturn. Saturn is primarily a god of agriculture, and through him concerns over time entered into this archetypal complex. In agriculture timing is crucial for planting and reaping. Kronos-Saturn brings with him an acute perception of time. In fact, this god's name has entered our language as a term for an inexorable, usually debilitating condition, something that is "chronic." But Kronos-Saturn also brings with him a sense of the appropriateness of timing, of needing to know "how things work," and of the necessity for an orderly, methodical approach to life. This archetypal pattern shapes our images of aging into stereotypical images when we think of old age as primarily a time of chronic, debilitating illness. In fact, there are more than a few elderly who lead active, productive and happy lives. Most of us are willing to admit some aspects of our unconscious tendency to stereotype the elderly, especially those aspects which we see as somehow "negative." Kronos-Saturn, however, presents a more subtle stereotype, subtle because of its benign nature, namely that of Wisdom. We look to our elderly to have learned from experience if not "book learning," and we want to call them "Wise

Old Men and Women." In many Native American societies the elders were in fact the keepers of the tribes' "wisdom." And in truth there are many older people who have indeed matured and grown "In wisdom and grace." But there are also many who have not, people who at best parrot conventional wisdom and at worst are downright silly. In this respect a random sample of senior citizens would probably be similar to a random sample of 40 year old people. To think otherwise is to be under the sway of the archetypal complex of Kronos-Saturn.

7.

Understanding the human reality of stereotyping can lead to genuine humility based upon a profound experience of human nature. Normally we like to think that we are in control of life. We have a sense of who we are, the ego. The ego needs to feel its own power and existence on a daily basis, so it continuously asserts itself, even claiming more credit than is due. One of its little tricks to maintain its illusion of power is to judge itself better than others. The more people it judges as inferior, the better the ego feels about itself. The ego uses stereotypes to make itself feel superior to whole groups of people, or so it would like to believe. In reality stereotyping can become one of the ego's most powerful nemeses, because in the process of stereotyping a group or even one individual person, some archetype of the collective unconscious quietly but effectively overpowers the conscious ego and asserts its own autonomous power. Of course in a rational moment, our egos don't believe that all the elderly are decrepit, yet that stereotype sneaks in and shapes our lives. Thus the ego is faced with the reality of its true condition—that it is a tiny part of our psychic reality, a small island floating on a vast psychic sea. Ultimately becoming aware of our stereotyping is a splendid opportunity for personal and interpersonal growth, for these stereotypes can be overcome only by a long, often difficult process of self-examination and growth in consciousness, and/or by a truly open and human contact with the person who is the target of our stereotype. This difficult growth in awareness will bring us closer to understanding and living our true natures, and that is the beginning of genuine humility.

8.

Lessons Learned from Aging

1.

Weaving is a marvelous art, a magical one. Imagine moving the shuttle to and fro, now brown thread, now yellow. Each individual line resting in its own place, each group of lines hardly more than the most abstract of patterns, yet a pattern develops. How does the weaver see this? Does she stand back at intervals like some painter at her canvas? Does he see the pattern instinctively, or does he pre-figure it in tiny mathematical intervals? And what about the untutored viewer of the finished piece? It is only with a proper distance that we see pattern unfold.

Writing a book can be a bit like weaving. Each chapter looks at a specific set of images, takes them apart, plays with their individual colors. But is there a pattern, an overall direction or theme to the work? If there is, it can only be seen from the perspective of a kind of distance. In this chapter we shall re-examine some of the topics of this book in order to discover an overall theme or direction. We shall attempt to discover the lessons learned from aging.

2.

We studied the power of remembering. My grandfather's stories, Tony's memories of Italy, these and others spoke of the value of life. They indicated that each and every event in life carries with it a great importance, one that reaches much further than the event itself. Bill's dreams and Martha's wanderings explored how the importance and meaning of the events of life, reside in the power these events have to move our inner lives. They showed me that I am going through life weaving the pattern of that life, much as a novelist would weave the text-ure of his characters' lives. In each encounter with another person, with each act and thought, in each moment of awareness and reflection, we are weaving our own personal myth and are simultaneously contributing to the greater myth that our society, in fact, all of humanity is collectively weaving. Our individual actions are not only important because of the results they produce, but because of their being part of these patterns of meaning and creation. Remembering brings these dimensions to consciousness.

Remembering—a memory—is the beginning of a powerful process which takes a literal, material event and brings it into the world of the imaginal, the world of symbols. In doing so remembering returns us to our true selves, to that identity which is normally hidden beneath the 10,000 distractions of everyday life.

In sharing the remembering of these many people, we have come to learn of a basic paradox in human life. In weaving and reweaving the elements of our lives we slowly come to the realization that this world is not entirely our "home." The more we come to value the people and things of this life, the more we also see that they are channels for some most profound reality. Thus all of life is a symbol, drawing us forward, out of ourselves, out of ego-centered worlds. The more we appreciate and value this world, the more we realize that it is also a guidepost and inspiration for our souls on their journey to Home.

3.

We learned about the power of silence. Frederica, Walter and Louis personified our tendency to perceive silence as an emptiness, and our dread of that feeling of void. They showed us the extreme to which we go to avoid silence, to fill the emptiness with any kind of noise, and how this noise isolates us from other people and keeps us from a confrontation and reconciliation with our inner reality. It is a strange paradox—that noise seems to allay one's anxieties about loneliness and emptiness but actually exacerbates one's isolation, thus making one feel more lonely. We also examined how our needs are manipulated to create desires for products and services less designed to fulfill our deepest needs than to make a profit by exacerbating them. Fred, Walter, Bill and Yolande presented a picture of silence as a transformative power in our lives. Not only can it refresh and restore an otherwise harried soul, but it can also be a doorway to an experience of the deepest mysteries of our being. Indeed, it can lead us to our true selves. In silence one can begin to contemplate, to peer into the vast unknown within and without. We have seen in the lives of these people how central silence and contemplation are to human life.

Silence—at first feared as a vast emptiness. In truth the real fear is that we ourselves are empty, nothing. But slowly silence shows its other face, and our other facets. Silence becomes the mystery out of which everything originates and to which everything returns. Our thoughts, our words even our bodies come from this Emptiness and return to It. And, in fact, we carry It around with us day in and day out, or perhaps It carries us within Itself. At any rate, silence teaches us that we are not what we think we are. In truth we "are" more mystery, more emptiness, we are more silence, than anything else.

4.

We learned of the importance of believing. We met people well acquainted with poverty, sickness and even death, people whose lives incarnated the absolute importance of believing in something, that is, in some meaning to life. What was written about the Jews in Hitler's concentration camps came alive in the streets of America, namely that one can "survive" anything, even cancer if meaning could be found in it. Denise, Annette and others like her taught us this as well as the fact that this basic human need is farther reaching than simply a survival mechanism. We discovered that this process of believing is one of the most fundamentally human of all activities.

The early years of life are spent building the personality. Slowly the ego comes to consciousness and asserts its power and territory. This assertion is, however, quite tenuous, and the ego constantly scans its environment for signs of affirmation or threat. A young child will be quick to interpret an adult's face as approving or disapproving. This is the beginning of the ego's work of assigning meaning to the world, and this rather primitive level of believing, primitive in the sense of its world view as either "for" or "against," will remain with each person for most of his or her life.

As we grow, however, the patterns of meaning and believing become more sophisticated. Each person develops his or her own philosophy of life, that is, we develop an understanding of how things are, how they should be and how we fit into that picture. Sometimes these are clearly individual beliefs. When they are shared by an entire community or even civilization they loose their obvious character as beliefs and seem to become hard fact. We have seen this in, for example, the difficulties that "new" thinkers have experienced. More than Copernicus and Galileo have been branded heretics. Frequently our own personal beliefs are held onto with an even tighter fist. For instance, even though one branch of science tells us that we are mostly water and another branch tells that we are energy vibrating at a different pulse, we stubbornly hold onto our beliefs that we are solid, physical beings. The corollary to this is, of course, our belief that only physical, material things are "real."

We have learned from the lives of countless seniors that if a person is true to him or her self, something will happen to crack open that personal belief in the importance of the physical, material world. Frequently this comes as a gradual suspicion that there is something "more." Occasionally it comes in the shock of an illness or a sudden vision or paranormal experience. Once it comes, and if we take it seriously, this "openning" will teach us that all of reality is primarily symbolic, that each experience and object will lead us further and further into the Unknown. Soon we will realize that our ideas are indeed our own constructs. They are necessary for our growth and development at certain stages but they also can keep us from seeing things as they really are. We also learn that "I" am not at all identical to "Ego," that "I" am a symbol for some Mystery. As we pursue life and our world as primarily symbolic, we are lead deeper and deeper into direct contact with Reality until these symbols, no longer necessary, fade away and we are "face to face" with whatever Is. Indeed it may be more accurate to say that we are lead to the realization that "I" and "Ultimate Reality" no longer exist, but there is only "Is."

5.

We have come to understand the importance of dance, both real and metaphorical. Some dances are slow and stately, some dark and passionate, some light and frisky. And so is life. In fact, life is a dance, expecially in terms of rhythm and timing. Life has its own seasons and rhythms, patterns. A right word spoken at the wrong time does little good. We discovered that even depression had its own sense of timing. Try as hard as possible, people just can't shake depression until its time is ripe. Relationships have their rhythms and patterns, dancing between closeness and distance, altruism and selfishness, etc. In fact, the thread running through all of this is that people like Josh showed us that all of life is nothing more or less than a dance. In other words, it is a series of themes and variations on these themes, woven and rewoven in different patterns, sounded by different instruments at different times. People like Jaroslav and Estrellita made it clear that it is futile to attempt to hold on to any one moment, or even to any one set pattern or identity. Life is a texture of patterns and myths. We are not one, a monolithic being, equal to our ego identity.

Rather we are a harmony of diverse elements, playing together, playing with and through the conscious personality. In fact, what seems to be most solid in life—our very bodies—is but vibrating energy.

The universe is a cosmic dance. For centuries mystics have held this view, and non-mystics have dismissed it as mere poetry. Now non-New-tonian physics is shaking up even the most hard nosed skeptic. But, really, one does not need to take classes in the history of religion or in particle physics to understand this reality. One simply needs to look at life reflec-tively, to see its patterns develop, shift and reconfigure. Exploring mo-ments from the lives of the elderly has amply illustrated that a touch of humor and some clear-eyed honesty is all that's needed to begin the Dance.

6.

Finally, we learned much about loving. In a dirty old man's sexual frustration we discovered the sexuality of the imagination. We learned how the mind animates the body through its images and fantasies. We came to appreciate that intimacy has more to do with one person's imagination fer-tilizing another person's imagination, and being fertilized in return, than with a physical act of potentially procreative dimensions. And in meeting couples like Robert and Julie, and from hearing of Maurice's powerful near-death encounter, we came to appreciate that the emotional, physical and imaginal qualities of life and sex can not be divided and separated. Any onesided leaning is, practically speaking, the beginning of its own corrective mechanism.

The sex drive seems, at least at times, unquenchable. And at times we seem to have an almost infinite ability to love as well as, perhaps, an equally large need to be loved. In fact, loving moves us to greater loving. There is no stopping, no end point. If we follow our natural inclination towards loving, we will open to greater and greater dimensions, to infinity. Our yearning and need for this experience teaches us that our true nature is an infinitely expanding force of life, a force we perceive as loving, and that we are but travellers passing through this world of ours. We live a paradox in that even though we are in this world, as embodied beings with physical bodies and emotional souls, we can remember, even fleetingly, our Home. This Home is not a different physical location or temporal lifetime. Rather it is a quality of consciousness available to us at each and every moment. The Beyond of Buddhism is right here, if I have eyes to see and ears to hear, and loving will point the way.

7.

There seem to be two themes unifying these diverse lessons learned from working with the elderly and reflecting upon that work and their lives. First of all, human life is situated in a "place in-between." We are not simply physical beings, tied to mother earth and the matter from which we are made. On the other hand we are not pure spirit, free to roam about at will through time and space. We are both physical and immaterial, simultaneously living in both realms, or more accurately living in a place in-between both realms.

We experience our in-betweenness most completely at those moments when we are most fully alive. These are the moments of our peak functioning, moments which Abraham Maslow called "peak experiences." (Maslow, 1967) For instance, I may be walking down the street and I become aware of the beautiful play of the autumnal sun on green-gold leaves. Somehow I feel changed. I feel a perfect harmony within myself and with this environment. My walking has a special effortless harmony. I feel the sun playing on my skin just as it plays on the leaves. Even the playful shouts of children and the noise and motion of a passing automobile seems to fit in so perfectly. And the harmony I feel is a harmony not just with this tiny scene but somehow with all of the world, the cosmos. These experiences can occur while viewing a sunrise, a sunset, a gentle drizzle, a child at play, a fireplace, while reading, making love, gardening, at practically any place and any time. I remember someone saying that Martin Heidegger defined a person as an opening through which the Absolute can manifest. It is at these moments of heightened awareness that we become most aware of our place in-between spirit and matter.

The second theme has to do with one of the unique ways in which our in-between nature manifests itself to us, namely that the human life is also the symbolic life. As previously indicated, it is important to distinguish a symbol from a sign. A sign has one clear "meaning" which it represents. A traffic sign indicates the activity of stopping, or going, etc. A symbol, on the other hand, does not simply convey information. A symbol is an image which also conveys the living reality of what it symbolizes. A wedding ring is not simply a sign of a marriage. After 20 years of shared life, that ring recreates those moments of joy, frustration, elation, love, etc.

In the pages of this book we examined how six aspects of daily life—remembering, silence, believing, dancing, loving and stereotyping—are symbolic activities. The central lesson learned in these discussions is that the manner in which the fully alive person realizes the most distinctively human aspect of his or her nature, namely that of a being in-between, is by daily living in contact with the images of the symbolic life.

8.

Working with the elderly also suggests a few reflections about lifestyle. The lessons learned in this work suggest that in order to live a happy and fully alive life, the symbolic life of an "in-between being," we must integrate the following points into our daily lives.

First of all, we need to live as much as possible in the present moment. This sounds simple, but in fact is rather difficult to do. Much of non-sleeping time is spent in the past or the future. Reminiscence differs from day-dreaming about the past. Day-dreaming is mostly an unconscious activity. Reminiscence brings a reflective awareness to the past, building a sense of interiority, of soul, by using our memories as symbols. Day-dreaming about the future, as opposed to consciously planning or fantasizing, usually does little more than reinforce our own neediness. One of the effects of living in the present is to build an openness which will be a source of joy and ecstacy as well as a source of sorrow and pain, for it will expose us to the multiple dimensions of life as it is lived around us and on this planet. As we become moved by our own sufferings and the sufferings and struggles of others, our openness can become a powerful and never depleting source of compassion.

If we are to live the symbolic life, we must learn to live a life of interiority. Unlike signs which usually shout their messages, symbolic images are normally shy and reserved beings. Their power is not in a message but in their operations upon one's inner life. In order to allow these images to accomplish their tasks, we need to stop our frenetic pace. We need leisure and times of silence, times of introversion, of directing our attention inward. Unfortunately this attitude is diametrically opposed to the frenetic, extroverted life style of the modern world, a world in which everything is, or will be, knowable and do-able. Yet symbols quietly cry out of the mysteries of life and the Mystery behind or beyond them. To fulfill our humanity we must take time and heed their cry.

Finally, we must learn to live with paradox. The simplest way of stating this is to say that nothing is ever what it seems to be. For instance, something I do to make myself feel good actually exacerbates my deepest wounds. A seemingly heartless act becomes a great moment of compassion. The reality of human life, that strange mixture of spirit and matter, is that, at each and every moment, many realities are occurring simultaneously. Understanding this requires a certain flexibility of mind, again a trait opposed to the trends of our current culture. Today we want hard facts, a by-product of our materialistic society, and the machines we use to process facts can deal with only "yes or no" statements. And as life becomes faster and faster, and more complicated and ambiguous, we look for a simple way out. And yet the glorious truth of human nature is that we are multi-dimensioned, symbolic beings. Life is a mystery in that life *isn't* what it usually appears to be. At the very heart of its being is a pulsing and dynamic Mystery.

9.

Working with Images

1.

We have examined and reflected upon many images, both from the lives of older adults and from the writings of many authors. The question still remains, how do I make use of these insights in my own life, or in my relationships with those I love and with whom I work?

This chapter will begin to answer the question, how do I work with images? While some of the following sections will be addressed to the professional helping person, the counselor, nurse, clergy, etc., the information presented is by no means only for these people. Anyone interested in working with the images, symbols, and metaphors of his or her own life can find direction and inspiration in the words which follow.

Frances Vaughn has written about the very important distinction between the content of therapy and its context. (Vaughn, 1980) The content is the subject matter discussed, and includes the techniques and interventions of the therapist. The context is more subtle but equally important. The context of therapy is more than just the physical setting of the encounter. It is primarily the mind-set of the therapist. There is an old saying that is relevant to this discussion, namely, you can't give what you don't have. A therapist who does not believe in the reality of the unconscious will not help a client understand the workings of his or her life as manifestations of the unconscious. A therapist who defines therapy as primarily relief from a symptoms's pain will not look into the meaning of that symptom or the part that it plays in a person's psychic economy. And most importantly, a therapist who does not have easy commerce with the power of images and symbols in his or her own life will not be able to work effectively with clients in an imaginal or symbolic mode.

Working with images and symbols leads us directly to transpersonal context. Images and symbols point beyond themselves, beyond the narrow confines of our ego centered life. We come to realize that, paradoxically, we are most ourselves when realities much greater than ourselves are playing through us. The word "personality" is derived from the mask worn by actors in the ancient theater, a mask which had a built in megaphone. That is the original meaning of the word "personality," a word composed of the words "per" and "sonare." "Sonare" means "to sound" and "per" means "through." Our personality is, therefore, on one level the presentation of our identities as act-ors in our lives and, on a deeper level, our personality is the instrument through which a "higher" dimension becomes manifest in our world. Some have called that "higher" dimension Archetype, others Being, Consciousness, the Higher Self, the Divine, etc. Image, as metaphor and symbol, is one of the primary means we have to come to an experiential understanding of that Reality.

Thus it is necessary for a therapist to actively work with the images present in his or her own life in order to help clients work with the images contained in their dreams, actions and symptoms. This is, of course, why a therapist's own therapy is most important. Also useful are various techniques of working with symbolic material, techniques which amount to what Jung called active imagination, in other words, a direct engagement of the ego with the images of the unconscious in an effort to value them and to lessen the controlling, though illusory, grip of the ego. (cf. works by Berry, Johnson, Kelsey and von Franz.) The next few sections will include some of my favorite techniques for working with images, but we must also consider one other very important aspect of the context of imaginal or archetypal therapy, namely that therapy or healing itself has a transpersonal dimension which it images in the myths of Chiron, the Wounded Healer.

Chiron was a centaur wounded by an arrowshot. He spent the remainder of his life pursuing a cure for his uncurable wound. In this process, Chiron discovered the secrets of healing all of humankind's diseases. The wounded Chiron became the wounded healer, and by his wound we are healed. Chiron passed his knowledge of the lore and craft of healing to Asclepius, who became the god of healing and whose shrines became the first wholistic hospitals.

Carl Jung wrote of the importance of this myth for modern times,

> We could say, without too much exageration, that a good half of every treatment that probes at all deeply consists in the doctor's examining himself, for only what he can put right in himself can he hope to put right in his patient. ...it is his own hurt that gives the measure of his power to heal. (Jung, C.W. 14:116)

In other words, each of us has within ourselves our own wounded healer. The central task of therapy is to learn to trust and activate our inner healer. This is accomplished in the supportive atmosphere of a human relationship in which one person, the therapist, trusts the power of images to lead to insight and healing. Thus the other person, the client, can learn to trust his or her own images.

This leaves us with two important implications. First of all, to the extent that a therapist is not in touch with his or her own wounded nature, the patient is seen as the only one with a "problem." The therapist thus carries all of the identity (and projections) as "healthy" and "healer." Thus anything which comes from within the "patient" is in some way tainted with pathology. How could a client work with and trust the images arising from one's depths? At best they can be trusted only after the approval and interpretation of the therapist. It would be a miracle that any relationship accepting of the inner life could be established in such a context.

Secondly, we must face the reality that the images arising within our clients will affect us also, sometimes quite powerfully. They will touch our own wounds and unconscious blind spots. They will present challenges to trust and love. And they will present opportunities for therapists, just as much as for clients, to allow the transpersonal to enter into and enliven life. Thus the context of therapy provides opportunities for tremendous regard for and gratitude to our clients, for they provide opportunities for our own growth and healing.

3.

If we are going to give careful attention to the images we find in our own lives as well as those which surface in our working with others, it is important to ask "What is an image?" It would seem obvious that an image is some kind of picture. Monet's haystacks are pictures, images he painted. But they are also something else. These pictures have a special power. Monet was not painting pictures of haystacks as much as he was painting his deeply felt impressions of the effects of light on the haystacks. These pictures are powerful because they are attempts to convey the ineffable, wonderous reality of light.

Images, especially if we approach them as psychological realities, are more than mere pictures. Images are functionally identical to symbols, that is they are the best possible representations of something as yet not fully known. If this is true of paintings, images which were created for a mostly conscious reason, how much more so true is it of the images which are the spontaneous creations of a person's unconscious!

This understanding of the nature of an image has important implications for our working with images. Mary Watkins summarizes these implications in her article, "Six approaches to the image in art therapy,"

We ask less "What does this image mean?" and more "What are the images intrinsic to the activities, thoughts, and feelings I am engaged in?" What images am I in when I feel exhausted, when I am shy or ambitious, when I am relating to my husband, child, or my own body? The image...lends us the imaginal background to each experience, thus raising the dayworld onto the plane of metaphorical meanings. As image and experience interpenetrate, the image is not discarded but becomes an eye through which one perceives and senses.... (The art therapist) is someone alert not just to the literal image which is drawn, but to images in the patients' gestures, tones of voice, ways of interacting, presenting complaints and history. Through this alertness she helps the patient interact with the image being expressed in order to see more metaphorically his or her daily struggles, fears, and preoccupations. (Watkins, 1981)

In other words, we will not approach images in order to "discover their meaning" i.e. to translate them from an imaginal to a seemingly more rational language. This is to treat images as signs not as symbols. Nor will we try to change or manipulate these images or parts of them, for they are, just as they are, the best possible representations of something at least partially unknown, and to tamper with the image will prevent our fuller experience of that unknown. Rather we will attempt to engage ourselves with the totality of the image, using it as if it were a pair of tinted eyeglasses to help us see our lives as metaphors.

Wanda was a faithful participant at her local senior center. She arrived each day at a few minutes past nine, poured herself a cup of coffee, went off to a quiet corner and spent the rest of the day knitting. She let it be known that she didn't want to talk with anyone and didn't want to participate in any activities. People let her have her own way, claiming that she just wasn't herself since her husband died, almost six years ago.

One day I was walking by and began a conversation, "Hi Wanda, what are you making?"

"Nothing much, I just like to sit here *by myself* and knit."

"You're pretty good at that. I'll bet you could even teach a class in knitting."

"Please don't try any of your social work stuff on me. I'm not depressed. I'm not going to commit suicide. My husband's dead and nothing can bring him back."

"It's ok, I wasn't even thinking of having you teach here. I don't think enough people would be interested. I was just admiring your work. I like the way you use colors. Not everyone has good color sense. Just look at the way you weave them together. Wanda, you're a real artist at that. You've got a real good sense of color."

Wanda shrugged off the compliment but it obviously hit home. About a week later she showed me a scarf she had designed with a carefully balanced color pattern of blues and reds. We talked for about half an hour, during which time the following occurred.

"You know, Wanda, when I think about colors, I think that a lot of times I choose certain colors because of the way I feel or because of the way they make me feel."

"I told you, I don't want any of that social work stuff."

"Just hold on. Didn't you ever have a blue day? (She nodded.)

That's all I'm talking about. Some days are blue, some brown, some red."

Our conversation returned to knitting.

Three days later we chanced to meet at the coffee pot and Wanda mentioned in passing, "Today's a blue day."

A few days later she came up to me and said, "It's red today."

"A red hot momma?"

She laughed.

About a month later Wanda and I had a long conversation about the colors and moods of life. We spoke of how different days, even different moments of the same day could be filled with experiences of different moods. I mentioned that I thought we were weavers making a tapestry of our lives, weaving and reweaving the colors until we found the right design. Wanda said she often felt like a knitting needle in the hands of someone much greater. Soon Wanda once again began to socialize with the other seniors.

It was obvious that Wanda was depressed after the death of her husband. It was equally obvious that if I tried to be a "social worker" I would have failed like others before me. The crucial difference was that I was able to see that "knitting" was a central image in her life. It was almost as if she were incarnating one of the Fates, weaving, or in this variation knitting, human destiny. I offered Wanda some human support and the opportunity to allow herself to go deeper into her central image. This allowed Wanda to use her own metaphorical system to deal with some profound and painful aspects of life. We did not attempt to manipulate or translate any of these images. We allowed two people to experience them more fully.

4.

What does working with people on the level of the symbolic life "look like?" Let us focus for a few moments on the contents of a typical session of imaginal or archetypal therapy, realizing that it isn't necessary to be behind the closed doors of a therapist's office to have a soul-to-soul conversation with a friend or loved one.

In many respects a session of symbolic therapy differs little from a session in any other style of talk therapy. The major difference is, as we have seen, the attitude of the therapist. This attitude will shape the focus of attention of the therapy "hour." (I write "hour" because I have done much of my work at senior centers in passing encounters, viz. Wanda, above.) James Hillman, archetypal psychology's leading spokesman, explains the essence of this focus of attention.

> Experience is never raw or brute; it is always constructed by images which are revealed in the patient's narrations... all events are regarded from a dream-viewpoint, as if they were images, metaphorical expressions. (Hillman, 1983)

Our work will focus upon the images which constitute the inner reality of a person's life, regardless of whether these images present themselves as dreams, figures of speech or the activities of daily life. These images are the perspectives which shape a person's life. Therapy from an imaginal perspective will focus upon assisting the patient to work with these images in order to free them from being treated as literal, material objects. Therapy will free the person to experience the metaphorical dimensions of his or her life. We have already seen this style of work in the life of one elderly widow, Wanda. It might be useful to consider two more examples of this approach to the psyche at work in therapy.

Hilda was a chronic wanderer who exasperated her family and a string or doctors, nurses and social workers. Her family brought her to counseling as a last ditch effort to prevent institutionalization. If the symbolic approach to the psyche held true, then Hilda's wanderings had to have some pattern, some meaning beyond mere physical exercise. Indeed, Hilda wandered in a small area of the city in which she lived her entire life. She became confused and lost only when she was distracted, took a wrong turn and ended up in an unfamiliar area. Panic would then set in.

One day I accompanied Hilda on one of her walks, encouraging her to share her memories and stories with me. While passing a dress shop she spoke of her senior prom dress and the great time she had at the prom. At a jewelry store she spoke of her late husband's pride as he presented her with an engagement ring purchased at that store. The dime store soda fountain found Hilda talking about summer walks with her children and later grandchildren, stopping for lunch or ice cream at its counter. Thus the meaning of Hilda's walking began to surface. Hilda was re-membering the patterns of her life in a literalized fashion. She needed to connect to the metaphorical or symbolic dimensions of these images.

The next week I had Hilda build a small model of the area which she wandered each day. I then encouraged her to "walk" a small plastic figure through this city and relate stories as she did. After some initial reticence, Hilda began to reminisce in this more metaphorical, i.e. less literal, manner. Some stories were repeated session after session, and some stories and sequences were modified with each recounting. Hilda was weaving and reweaving the strands of her life, creating her own personal mythology. Soon one of Hilda's grandchildren joined our sessions. She was fascinated by her grandmother's stories and began to tape record them. After a while other members of the family joined, all taking part in this family history project. Hilda also joined a senior's exercise group in order to eliminate some of the physical tension which her earlier walks dissipated. Within a few weeks Hilda's wandering had disappeared, replaced by a sophisticated act of the imagination, and her personal feelings of well being and happiness were at an all time high. Hilda's dementia slowly increased and eventually she had to be placed in a convalescent facility, but throughout the entire time Hilda and her family were able to maintain meaningful contact through the power of image and story.

Miriam came for counseling because she couldn't get over the sudden death of her husband, an event which occurred about 4 years before she came for help. She had previously been to a psychiatrist who prescribed an anti-depressant medication which Miriam refused to take because it left her too drowsy. It seemed to me that the central metaphors of Miriam's life were connected with her relationship to her husband, so I encouraged Miriam to begin an imaginal dialogue with him. After I reassured her that she was not "going crazy" Miriam began to dialogue with her husband, at first in my office but later in her own home as well. Soon she carried on a daily half-hour chat with him on topics ranging from chit-chat to advice on budgeting and plumbing to deep discussions of serious emotional issues. Soon Miriam resumed her old interest in oil painting and began to go to bingo with some of her old friends. Without medications or behavioral interventions, without interpretations and "symbology," Miriam broke through a 4 year cycle of depression and began to live life again. Miriam de-literalized the image of her husband, restored it to its rightful place in her imagination and entered into dialogue with it, thus metaphorically and psychologically relating to the parts of her psyche to which the image of her husband led her, or as we so clinically say, relating to the complexes in her unconscious.

5.

Understanding image as metaphor has certain implications for the techniques of therapeutic intervention. Once again, the foremost point is that the awareness of the therapist will largely determine the outcome of a "technique." For instance, a gestalt-style dialogue in which a person imagines that they are carrying on a discussion with a part of their inner life can be perfomed in order to exercise that inner dimension or to develop its metaphorical quality. There are, however, some techniques that seem to lend themselves to imaginal work more than other techniques. I have developed one of these techniques while working with my own symbolic material and call it "The 'Board of Directors' Meeting." It is a specific development of Jung's active imagination.

As we have seen in the chapter "On Stereotypes and Archetypes," each person's life is influenced by many archetypes, for instance, mother, father, child, martyr, anger (Mars), eros, etc. These archetypes manifest within the psyche by means of images. These images form the nucleus of each archetypal complex. They form the bodies and voices of the vast realms of our unconscious. It is possible to identify these images and to dialogue with them. We have just seen this in the story of Miriam's dialogue with the image of her departed husband. It is also possible to have one image dialogue with another. For instance, if Miriam would have recognized a small, hurt child within herself, the image of her husband could have dialogued with that of the child.

In the "Board of Directors' Meeting" a person identifies a group of recurrent images, usually 6 to 12 people, animals or things, and regularly calls them together for a meeting. "Guests," that is characters who are not regularly part of the group, can also be invited to attend. The image of the

"I" or the ego of the person serves as the Chairman of the Board and conducts the meeting.

John came to me because of difficulty he was experiencing in facing retirement. We worked together for about a year and a half during which time John developed his own Board of Directors. The first few weeks of therapy were focused upon John's complaints of feeling very old and worn out. In a guided imagination exercise, John visualized that part of himself as a worn out and depressed bag of bones type of old man. In his dreams, however, a young man of about 20 appeared, dressed in knight's armor and riding a white horse. As therapy continued John came to realize that within him also lived a Christian hermit; an overweight, brutal thug; a brown bear; a young, buxom harlot dressed in red; a mole; a woman of about 50 who was a talented musician; a drunken and sex-crazed reveler; and a clown. Each of these characters made regular appearances in his dreams, fantasies, thoughts, feelings or actions. They comprised his Board of Directors and met twice a week for about 45 minutes. One day John reported the following session:

I: I called you together for a special session and am very appreciative of your spending time with me today. The question at hand is the problem I'm having with Wilma, (John's wife) specifically about our not having a lot of romance and sex.

Harlot: Dump her, John, you can do better at any senior center. Hell, you can pick up a nice looking 40 yr. old and have a great fuck if you want. I'll help you. I need some good fucking.

Reveler: Yeah, baby, anytime you want it good and hard I'm ready.

Hermit: I truly feel sorry for these two, and for you John. You're missing the whole point of love. If you took your energies and offered to help someone you wouldn't have to worry about sex.

Reveler: Hey, fruitcake, you can take you rosary and...

I: Reveler stop. You know the ground rules. You can express yourself all you want but you must respect the being and opinion of all the others.

Reveler: I guess I overstepped my bounds. But Jesus, John, don't listen to this guy. You need a little piece now and then for your own health. Use it before you lose it.

Harlot: That's right, John, you haven't been paying much attention to your body lately. It deserves kindness and pleasure.

Musician: I don't think that sex is the real issue here. John, could you perhaps tell us a little more about how you're feeling about this problem with you and your wife?

I: (pause) Mostly unappreciated. A little lonely. And I feel very tense.

Thug: Like when I was beatin' on ya each night.

I: Well yes, almost like that.

Thug: Thought you'd get rid of me, huh?

(Everyone chuckles)

Mole: Let's dig into this a little deeper. Wilma's not your mother.

Clown: Even though you do like to suck her...

(Snickers)

I: I know she's not my mother, and I don't think I'm projecting nearly as much as I used to. But something is very wrong here.

Knight: Have you done anything to show her how special she is to you?

Bear: Like hugged her or maybe spent time with her watching a sunset?

The dialogue continued for almost 45 minutes, and as it continued and deepened John was able to look at his life from the perspective of each of his inner characters. He discovered the image or metaphor present in the difficulty with his wife by discovering where he was creating imbalance by becoming fixed in one or two images to the painful neglect of others. This time he even received specific advice as to what in his behavior needed to be modified, advice which was very successful in correcting the difficulties he was experiencing with his wife.

6.

Amplification is a very useful technique for opening the heart of an image. Amplification comes from the verb "amplify," meaning to make something louder. When we amplify an image we make the heart of the image, its core or essence, a little louder so that the dull "ears" of our psyche can hear it. This technique is easily abused. It is tempting to "associate to" the image thinking that "amplification" is taking place. For instance, in dealing with a depressed woman one can get the idea that this person is somehow acting out the patterns of depressed Demeter seeking Persephone, and produce slides, pictures, mythological texts and all sorts of "symbols and symbolic meanings." What usually happens, however, is that the depressed person gets more and more depressed, wondering about either the sanity of the "helping" person or accusing him or herself of being too stupid to see the point. The problem is that few, if any, of the associations went to the heart or core of the image. Amplification requires careful attunement to the central features of the image being considered in the total context of both the patient's life and the psyche's collective dimensions. Books of symbols are interesting distractions which can provide the illusion of working with symbols in a deeply psychological manner.

Amplification must amplify the heart of the image. Remember back to Wanda, the depressed lady who knitted all day. To speak to her of Demeter or of the Senex would be to miss the point. The central image in Wanda's life was so powerful and pervasive that it captured her entire being. Wanda spent all day *knitting*. Wanda needed to go deeper into that image which was so central to her life. The image's powerful energies were released when she faced the image with friendship and consciousness. My "intervention" was really an example of amplification.

Sometimes the image presents itself in a dream, sometimes in a lifestyle or behavioral pattern, sometimes in a physical or emotional symptom. We have seen an example of the amplification of a behaviorable image, let us first consider an example of a dream image and then one of a physical symptom image. Paul recorded the following dream:

> I was walking along a road which reminded me of Dorothy's path in the Wizard of Oz when I was struck from behind so hard that I fell down. The next thing I knew I was in a wild west town. I ordered a glass of milk and some guy called me a wimp and punched me. The scene shifted to some sort of medieval castle dungeon, at least that's what I think it was. All I remember is waking up with my back all beaten and bloody.

This dream taught me, by trial and error, the importance of amplifying the heart of the dream. When we first discussed this dream I focused upon the road as a "symbol" of life's path or the path of individuation. The session ended on a particularly lifeless note. The dream still had a lot of charge for Paul, so we dealt with it in the next session. At first I focused upon the contrast between the wild west and the milk, attempting to "amplify" the images of a mother complex versus budding masculinity. It went nowhere, fast. Then I noticed that the dream image repeated three times the picture of his being beaten. I was so eager to get meaning out of, or perhaps in to, the dream that I had missed the fact that the image repeated itself three times. It was calling out in capital letters!

I asked Paul to allow the images of being beaten into his imagination. Soon a flood of pictures, feelings and memories poured like a torrent. He began by imagining himself tied to a pillar and being whipped. He remembered scenes of his mother beating him, fantasies which plagued him during masturbation and episodes of whoring, and he sensed how deep down his current job was like being beaten. As he turned, in his imagination, to face his tormentor, Paul learned that this thug was being paid by his (Paul's) own mother. Focusing upon and amplifying the heart of the image helped generate a tremendous amount of learning and eventual self-healing.

Sometimes the image presents itself as a physical symptom. No one works better with these images than Arnold Mindell, who said that the body is a dream waiting to happen. His books are filled with examples of this work. I would like to present one vignette from my case work to illustrate how symptoms are image-symbols. William was referred to me by his family physician. William complained of chronic difficulty in breathing although the best tests and techniques of modern medicine could find no physical reason for this difficulty. After we established rapport, I asked William to tell me what it was like not to be able to breathe. He placed his hands over his chest and said it was like a ton of bricks sitting on him. With his permission I then placed my hands over his chest and began to apply pressure. Nothing much seemed to be happening, so after a few minutes of considerable pressure I asked him to change places with me. He began to put pressure on my chest. He pressed harder and harder. Soon this previously dignified 62 year old gentleman was bearing down on me, shouting and cursing at full volume. William was certainly breathing freely! As he was pressing on me I asked him to remember any image, thought or feeling which crossed his mind. Later, in speaking about this exercise, William recounted experiencing a previously forgotten image of his father berating him as a youngster, predicting that William's life would end in a total failure. Now, shortly after William's retirement, his father metaphorically returned and was sitting on his son's chest. Amplifying the image present in the physical symptom helped William face with awareness what was going on in his unconscious. From that point on William reported almost total relief of his symptom, and when it did return, William took it as an indication that he needed to have a talk with his critical inner parent.

Amplifying the image in dream, action or symptom is an extremely powerful and effective technique for working with and deepening the symbolic life. It is particularly effective because it stays very close to the original image and assists us to go deeper into it. This movement into the image is the chief difference between amplification and association. Association, a process of allowing the image to resonate into other areas of our inner and outer lives, can be a very effective technique if used judiciously. Association can help bring the image into daily life and it can help a person to revision his or her problems from a more archetypal perspective, but it can also move a person farther away from the heart of the image, as we have seen in the example of Paul's dream. Let us end this section with an example of an effective use of association.

Claire was feeling very depressed, though she could not find a cause for her depression. She tried to dismiss it as "old age blues," but it continued to intensify. She spent most of her time at home, either sitting in a corner of the den or cleaning and recleaning her kitchen. I met Claire at her home, where she sat in the chair in the corner of her den, chain-smoking. After a while I asked her to tell me the first thing that came to her mind, whatever it was, when I mentioned something. She agreed. I said "kitchen" and "cleaning the kitchen" and she replied, "dirty, have to, mom hitting me, it's my job," and "I loved her." To my cue "mom" she replied, "caring, loving, always drunk, beating, loving," and "praying to Mary."

During the remainder of that session Claire came to see how much she was feeling unloved and lonely, and how this triggered unresolved hurt and anger at her mother. She also recounted how, as a child, she was comforted by a devotion to the Virgin Mary. Over the course of a few weeks Claire was able to release some of her anger, begin to form new friendships, and renew a religious devotion which became a source of strength and comfort. Claire's associations helped her to bring the image she was enacting into her conscious life. They also helped her to situate herself in a larger transpersonal or archetypal context, drawing upon those energies for meaning and healing.

7.

We have now arrived at the end of this chapter and, indeed, the end of this book. Let us once more remind ourselves of the necessity of bowing our heads in a kind of psychological humility and allowing ourselves to learn from our images.

Marsilio Ficino was one of the primary shapers of the Italian Renaissance. Ficino inspired the hearts and minds of thinkers, politicians and artists with a lofty picture of the ideals of a humanism firmly rooted in an understanding of Plato. Where did Ficino learn his Plato? Not in the universities or seminaries, but in his own study. Night after night Ficino spoke with Socrates, Plato and others. He questioned their thoughts and ideas and they challenged his. But, you say, they had been dead for centuries before the birth of this scholar-physician-priest. Surely you mean that Ficino studied their writings from newly discovered scrolls. No, Ficino *spoke with* Plato and others, and nightly at that. Ficino allowed their images to form in his imagination with such intensity that he learned philosophy from them. This is not any more strange or different from Miriam (above) learning plumbing or check-balancing from the image of her husband. It simply requires that the ego swallow a bit of its omnipotent pride.

When we are honest with ourselves, we admit that the most powerful and profound images in our lives are not of our own making. They come to us, or we come upon them, more as discoveries or gifts, sometimes even unwanted. It is equally true that if we remain faithful to these images they will teach us the marvels of our selves and our universe. They will indeed transform us.

Sometimes an image will burst forth in a revelation of its meaning. Most of the time these images require constant nurturing care. Like a good sauce, they need to be put on the back burner, to be lived with day in and day out until one can no longer tell the difference between the image and the self. They then become like a new pair of eyes, and everywhere we look we see their images in place of the images created by our egos to maintain the illusion of power and control. Sometimes images require hard reflection, even to the point of determining the direction and content of our reading. But always they are there, lively participants in an ongoing discussion, teasing, coaxing, gesticulating, pointing. We can learn from these images and as we do, we can feel ourselves deepen and broaden. We can begin to feel something, or someone, being created deep within our souls, and in talking with our images we come to discover that that something or someone is the elusive *aurum non vulgum,* the gold at the end of the alchemists' quest. In learning from our images, we will discover the reality of our souls.

Bibliography

Berry, P. *Echo's Subtle Body*. Dallas: Spring Publications, 1982.

Campbell, J. *The Mythic Image*. Princeton: Princeton U. Press, 1974.

Casals, P. *Joys and Sorrows*. New York: Simon and Schuster, 1970.

Casey, E. Getting placed. "Spring," 1982.

de Chardin, T. *Hymn of the Universe*. New York: Harper & Row, 1958.

Courbin, H. *Avicene and the Visionary Recital*. Dallas: Spring Publ., 1980.

Dickey, J. *Poems 1957-1967*. Middletown, CT.: Wesleyan U. Press, 1978.

Eliot, T.S. *Four Quarters*. New York: Harcourt, Brace, Jovanovich, 1943.

Ficino, M. *The Book of Life*. Dallas: Spring Publ., 1980.

Grof, C. & Grof, S. Spiritual emergency—the understanding and treatment of transpersonal crises. "ReVision," 1986, V.8 No. 2.

Gustafson, F. The black madonna of Einsiedeln. A paper presented to the Analytical Psychology Club of Chicago, Jan. 4, 1976. Transcript courtesy of the author.

Hillman, J. An inquiry into image. "Spring," 1977.

_____ *Pothos:* The nostalgia of the puer eternus. *Loose Ends.* Zurich: Spring Publ., 1975.

_____ *Re-visioning Psychology.* New York: Harper & Row, 1975.

Hoffman, Y. *Japanese Death Poems.* Rutland, VT: Charles E. Tuttle Co., 1986.

Huxley, A. *Collected Essays.* New York: Harper & Row, 1958

Jung, C.G. *Memories, Dreams, Reflections.* New York: Vintage Books, 1963.

The Collected Works. Bollingen Series XX. Princeton: Princeton U. Press.

  The Structure and Dynamics of the Psyche. (vol. 8, 2nd. ed.) 1968.

  Civilization in Transition, (vol. 10, 2nd, ed.) 1970.

  Psychology and Religion: East and West, (vol.11, 2nd. ed.) 1968.

  Mysterium Conjunctionis, (vol 14, 2nd. ed.) 1970.

Kelsey, M. *Discernment.* New York: Paulist Press, 1978.

Kerenyi, K. *The Gods of the Greeks.* London: Thames and Hudson, 1951.

Lamb, F.B. *Wizard of the Upper Amazon.* Berkeley, CA: North Atlantic Books, 1971.

Leonard, G. *The Silent Pulse.* New York: E.P. Dutton, 1978.

Nouwen, H. *The Way of the Heart.* New York: Seabury Press, 1981.

MacLeish, A. *J.B.* New York: Samuel French, Inc. 1958.

Maslow, A. *Towards a Psychology of Being.* Princeton: Van Nostrand, 1962.

Mindell, A. *Working with Examining the Body*. Boston: Routledge & Kegan Paul, 1985.

Picard, M. *The World of Silence*. Gateway Editions, Ltd., 1952.

Porphyry. *De Antra Nympharum*. Buffalo, NY: S.U.N.Y., 1969.

Rilke, R.M. *Rilke on Love and Other Difficulties*, New York: W.W. Norton & Co., 1975.

Tarthang Tulku, *Hidden Mind of Freedom*. Berkeley, CA: Dharma Press, 1981.

Sarton, M. *Journal of a Solitude*. New York: W.W. Norton & Co., 1973.

Scott-Maxwell, F. *The Measure of My Days*. New York: Penguin Books, 1981.

Sontag, S. *Under the Sign of Saturn*. New York: Random House, 1981.

Stein, M. *"The Devouring Father"*. In Berry, ed. *Fathers & Mothers*. Zurich: Spring Publ., 1973.

Stovich, R. *Psychology and Salvations: A Reflection Upon the Human Condition*. "Chicago Studies," 1982, 21.

Vaughan, F. Transpersonal Therapy: Context, Content and Process. In Walsh & Vaughan, eds. *Beyond Ego*. Los Angeles: J.P. Tarcher, Inc., 1980.

Watkins, M. *Six Approaches to the Image in Art Therapy*. "Spring," 1981.

Yeats, W.B. "The old men admiring themselves in the Water." In Sanders, et. al. *Chief Modern Poets of England and America*. New York: The Macmillan Co., 1976.

*A commercially recorded audiocassette containing the visualizations and meditations found in this book, along with appropriate introductions and relaxation routines, is available by mail order. Using a prerecorded tape can make these exercises easier, more enjoyable and more profitable. For each copy of this tape, please send a check or money order for $7.95 plus $.55 postage and handling (total $8.50), payable to RAYMOND J. STOVICH, Ph.D., mailed to:

RAYMOND J. STOVICH, PH.D.
CENTERPOINT PUBLICATIONS
P.O. BOX 9465
SAN JOSE, CA 95157-0465

7762-9
5-05